dekalog

THE NEW HOME FOR SERIOUS FILM CRITICISM

The *Dekalog* series is a new list of bi-annual publications, released each March and September, dedicated to presenting serious and insightful criticism on a wide range of subjects across the full spectrum of contemporary global cinema.

Each issue is a guest-edited specially-themed volume including the writings of a diverse collection of authors, from academic scholars and cultural theorists, film and media critics, and filmmakers and producers, to various personalities involved in all kinds of institutionalised cinephilia such as film festival directors, cinema programmers and film museum curators.

The intention, therefore, is to include the multiple voices of informed and complementary commentators on all things cinematic in dedicated volumes on subjects of real critical interest, especially those not usually served by established periodicals or book-length publications.

In addition to specially commissioned essays, each issue also includes an exclusive '*Dekalog* Interview' with a leading figure related to the theme in question, and a '*Dekalog* Re-View' section where readers' feedback will be edited by respective guest editors and published in subsequent editions. All readers are therefore very much invited to participate in the discussions by contacting any of the series' guest editors on dekalog@wallflowerpress.co.uk

ALSO AVAILABLE IN THE *DEKALOG* SERIES:

Dekalog 1: On The Five Obstructions
guest edited by Mette Hjort

Dekalog 2: On Manoel de Oliveira
guest edited by Carolin Overhoff Ferreira

FORTHCOMING ISSUES IN THE *DEKALOG* SERIES:

Dekalog 4: On East Asian Filmmakers
guest edited by Kate Taylor

Dekalog 5: On Dogville
guest edited by Sara Fortuna & Laura Scuriatti

dekalog³
On Film Festivals

GUEST EDITOR: RICHARD PORTON

WALLFLOWER
LONDON & NEW YORK

First published in Great Britain in 2009 by
Wallflower Press
6 Market Place, London W1W 8AF
www.wallflowerpress.co.uk

A catalogue record for this book is available from the British Library.

ISBN 978-1-906660-06-2 (pbk)

Printed in the UK by Cromwell Press Group, Trowbridge, Wiltshire

Contents

Notes on Contributors   vii

INTRODUCTION: ON FILM FESTIVALS   1
Richard Porton

I. A BACKWARD GLANCE
THE FESTIVAL VIEWED AS A RELIGIOUS ORDER   11
André Bazin

II. FILM FESTIVALS: BETWEEN ART AND COMMERCE
FIRST YOU GET THE POWER, THEN YOU GET   23
THE MONEY: TWO MODELS OF FILM FESTIVALS
Mark Peranson

THE FESTIVAL GALAXY   38
Quintín

THE SANDWICH PROCESS: SIMON FIELD TALKS ABOUT   53
POLEMICS AND POETRY AT FILM FESTIVALS
James Quandt

CINEPHILIA AND FILM FESTIVALS   81
Robert Koehler

HERE AND ELSEWHERE (THE VIEW FROM AUSTRALIA)   98
Adrian Martin

III. MEMOIRS AND CASE STUDIES
ASIAN FILM FESTIVALS AND THEIR DIMINISHING   109
GLITTER DOMES: AN APPRAISAL OF PIFF, SIFF AND HKIFF
Stephen Teo

THE SAD CASE OF THE BANGKOK FILM FESTIVAL   122
Kong Rithdee

STATUS QUO AND BEYOND: THE VIENNALE,   131
A SUCCESS STORY
Christoph Huber

BAGATELLE FOR KINO OTOK AND I 1000 OCCHI   143
Olaf Möller

SOME FESTIVALS I'VE KNOWN: A FEW   151
RAMBLING RECOLLECTIONS
Jonathan Rosenbaum

IV. THE FILMMAKER'S PERSPECTIVE
A DIRECTOR ON THE FESTIVAL CIRCUIT: 169
AN INTERVIEW WITH ATOM EGOYAN
Richard Porton

THE *DEKALOG* RE-VIEW   183

Notes on Contributors

Christoph Huber was born in 1973 in Vöcklabruck and studied at the Technical University of Vienna. He lives in Vienna and is active as a film writer, mainly as the chief critic for the daily paper *Die Presse*. Author of programme notes for the Austrian Film Museum and contributing editor for *Cinema Scope*, he regularly contributes to various film books and magazines around the world.

Robert Koehler is a film critic for *Variety*, *Cinema Scope* and *Cineaste*. A former theatre critic for the *Los Angeles Times*, he has also written reviews, articles and essays for a number of publications including *Cahiers du cinéma* and *Die Tageszeitung*. He is a member of FIPRESCI and has served on juries at various festivals, including Cannes, Vancouver, Buenos Aires, Mexico City, Slamdance, Guadalajara, Palm Springs, Los Angeles Latino, San Francisco Latino, Los Angeles Polish and Bermuda. His occasional blogs on cinema can be read at Filmjourney.org. As a member of the Los Angeles Film Critics Association, he serves on the Experimental/Independent award committee, which annually recommends to LAFCA membership the best experimental or independent film that screened in Los Angeles during the past year.

Adrian Martin is Senior Research Fellow in Film and Television Studies at Monash University (Australia). For 11 years he reviewed films for *The Age* (Melbourne) and is co-editor of the online journal *Rouge*. His books include *Once Upon a Time in America* (1998), *The Mad Max Movies* (2003), *Raul Ruiz* (2004) and *Movie Mutations* (2003), which he co-edited with Jonathan Rosenbaum

Olaf Möller was born, raised and is still living in Cologne, Germany. He writes about and programmes films. His column 'Olaf's World' appears in *Film Comment*.

Mark Peranson is editor and publisher of *Cinema Scope* and programming coordinator for the Vancouver International Film Festival. He recently completed *Waiting for Sancho*, an experimental documentary on the making of Albert Serra's *El cant dels ocells* (*Birdsong*).

James Quandt has been Director of Programming and then Senior Programmer at Cinematheque Ontario, Toronto since 1990, where he organised major touring retrospectives of the films of Robert Bresson, Kenji Mizoguchi, Kon Ichikawa, Shohei Imamura, Mikio Naruse and Nagisa Oshima, and edited accompanying monographs on Bresson, Ichikawa and Imamura. He is a regular contributor to *Artforum*.

Quintín is former editor of the monthly film journal *El Amante Cine*, and former director of the Buenos Aires International Film Festival.

Kong Rithdee has written film criticism for 13 years for *The Bangkok Post*, Thailand's leading English-language newspaper. He also contributes to the Thai-language magazine *Nang Thai*, published by the Thai Film Foundation, and to *Bioscope* magazine.

Jonathan Rosenbaum, for many years the film critic for *The Chicago Reader*, is also a regular contributor to *Cinema Scope*, and has also published widely in other newspapers and magazines such as *The Village Voice*, *Sight and Sound*, *Film Comment* and *Cineaste*. His books include monographs on *Greed* (1993) and *Dead Man* (2000); *Moving Places* (1980), *Placing Movies* (1995), *Movies as Politics* (1997), *Essential Cinema* (2004) and *Discovering Orson Welles* (2007). His website, which features reviews, articles and a blog, is at jonathanrosenbaum. com.

Stephen Teo is currently associate professor at the Wee Kim Wee School of Communication, Nanyang Technological University, Singapore. Prior to joining NTU, he was a research fellow at the Asia Research Institute, National University of Singapore from 2005–08. He is the author of *Hong Kong Cinema: The Extra Dimensions* (1997), *Wong Kar-wai* (2005), *King Hu's 'A Touch of Zen'* (2007) and *Director in Action: Johnnie To and the Hong Kong Action Film* (2007).

Introduction:
On Film Festivals

Richard Porton

It is difficult to pinpoint why film festivals trigger confessional impulses in critics saddled with the responsibility of writing about these intermittently gratifying, frequently maddening, events. In the anthology you are about to read, one article is an outright memoir while several of the others include lengthy autobiographical interludes. In some respects, film festival communiqués can be considered a form of travel writing. Yet instead of producing Baedekers chronicling famous sites in foreign climes, the best festival reports inevitably chart quasi-Proustian journeys into the interior. The films viewed in marathon sessions are occasionally, like Proust's madeleines, conduits of bliss. All too often, however, they merely resemble stale biscuits. In any case, for the travelling, but necessarily sedentary, cinephile, describing the contradictory bundle of experiences engendered by most film festivals is profoundly personal.

The importance of harnessing the personal (although hopefully non-narcissistic) voice was uppermost in my mind while commissioning the essays, memoirs, interviews and impassioned polemics included in this volume. This priority was at least partially designed to offer a distinctive alternative to the largely pedestrian film festival reports found in newspapers and even film magazines – as well as the decidedly uneven commentary on film festivals that has appeared in book form in recent years. Most of the writing on festivals by mainstream critics is inordinately celebratory. To a certain extent, this is attributable to the fact that magazine festival reports, even in highbrow journals, are at least partially written as 'payback' – for either airfare, accommodations, or in the case of the snootier festivals, the mere privilege of receiving accreditation and standing in interminable queues. A panel sponsored by FIPRESCI (the International Federation of Film Critics) at the 2008 Oberhausen International Short Film Festival introduced the possibility that critics risk surrendering their integrity and losing their independence by becoming 'embedded' within the industry and the festival circuit. Even a book such as Kenneth Turan's *Sundance to Sarajevo: Film Festivals and the World They Made* (2002), despite some accurate observations concerning the more gruelling aspects of attending Cannes and Sundance, is relentlessly upbeat – as well as essentially conformist in its aesthetic predilections. Turan, for example, chides Sundance for its supposed 'anticommercial bias', whereas Robert Koehler in his piece in this volume on cinephilia and film festivals castigates the same event as a 'horror show' that does everything in its ability to marginalise any vestige of innovative cinema while remaining obsessed with a facile, if marketable, brand of 'indie' filmmaking.

All of the somewhat jaundiced, but certainly not jaded, contributors to this volume view the myriad contradictions of the contemporary festival milieu with a bracingly ambivalent mixture of affection and informed revulsion. The pleasures of 'binging' on five or six films each day is often negated by the irksome feeling that one's 'coverage' is designed to prop up the edifice of a hollow spectacle. Major film festivals are now much more than venues for screening movies and encouraging camaraderie among cinephiles. Megafestivals such as Cannes, Toronto and Berlin have metamorphosed into ultra-hierarchical corporate entities in which the most glamorous, although not necessarily the most artistically distinguished, films are displayed in competitions that receive the lion's share of media attention while more audacious work is ghettoised in sidebars that are usually only covered with any depth by specialised film magazines. A fierce passion for the cinema tempered by a sober awareness of the threat of the economic bottom line and film festivals' version of realpolitik imbues many of these essays. Mark

Peranson's 'First You Get the Power, Then You Get the Money: Two Models of Film Festivals' examines 'festivals as political actors' while identifying the interest groups that now set the agenda for the international dissemination of art cinema. Even the realm of auteur cinema is now beholden to the vicissitudes of the market; Peranson identifies sales agents – a category 'that didn't exist a few decades ago' – as movers and shakers whose power nearly approaches the scope of government agencies. As a programmer at the Vancouver International Film Festival, an event known more for its innovative programming than for outsized glitz, Peranson comes down on the side of 'audience festivals' which attempt to serve the needs of the public during an era where the corporate model of the 'business festival' is becoming increasingly dominant.

Quintín, former director of the Buenos Aires International Festival of Independent Films (BAFICI) and former editor of *El Amante Cine*, provides an acerbic account of the contemporary film festival 'galaxy'. Railing against the bureaucratic mediocrity of many established festivals, Quintín unsurprisingly invokes the example of his four memorable years at BAFICI, a festival whose programming continues to reflect a cinephilic, critical sensibility, as an alternative to curatorial stodginess. It's certainly noteworthy that several of the other contributors pay explicit homage to BAFICI and Quintín's legacy inasmuch as his vision of a festival, suffused with what Jonathan Rosenbaum in his contribution to this book, 'Some Festivals I've Known', terms 'experimental notions' about programming, represents an antidote to the cautious efforts to please all constituencies (thereby frequently pleasing none) that plagues, among other events, Sundance, Cannes and Toronto.

There is perhaps an underlying anxiety, shared by critics, filmmakers and the public, that mega-festivals' burgeoning importance (or, perhaps more accurately, burgeoning self-importance) makes them paradoxically unfestive and preoccupied with maintaining their status as 'brands'. There are of course vestiges, even in corporate film festivals, of the transformative power of ancient rituals, allowing spectators to forget everyday banal woes and experience 'time out of time'.[1] On the other hand, the traditional liminality of festivals is difficult to discern in business festivals and often appears to have become transmogrified into pure spectacle. Many commentators, including the ones in this book, tend to implicitly consider certain festivals as either utopian or dystopian – while also fully aware that most of them fall in the middle of such a continuum.

For serious film critics, a cinephilic festival offers the most tangible *promesse de bonheur*. André Bazin's 1955 essay, 'The Festival Viewed as a Religious Order', which starts off this collection (making its first appearance in English) wittily compares the pilgrimage of critics to Cannes to an initiation into a monastic order – film writers come together from all corners of the globe to spend two weeks living a life diametrically opposed to their everyday professional and private existence' and descend upon the Riviera to worship a 'transcendent reality': the cinema. Yet Robert Koehler's contribution, 'Cinephilia and Film Festivals', asserts that 'any festival that matters has only one crucial task, and that is to defend cinema' – and he makes it clear that many festivals fail to pay adequate reverence to the cinematic muse. Peranson compares the seemingly infinite variety of contemporary film festivals to an efflorescence of Starbucks while Koehler reminds us that the Seattle International Film Festival was once labelled 'a kind of Wal-Mart of movies of any and all types that fit into some commercial category'. Even though the hegemony of the market may now seem like an irreversible process, the essay that follows Koehler's jeremiad, Adrian Martin's 'Here and Elsewhere (The View From Australia)', wryly points out that utopian schemes for film festivals sometimes congeal into lame pleas for institutional reform. To wit, Australian critic Lesley Stern's 1981 plea for freewheeling festivals that might be construed as 'moveable feasts' ends with a 'grimly ironic' plea for her agenda to be considered by the Australian Film Institute, a body Martin characterises as a 'relentlessly mainstream organisation'. One of the animating tensions of Koehler's article involves the way in which the institutional frameworks of festivals both converge and conflict with the cinephile's agenda. Film enthusiasts seemingly can't live with the conservative aesthetic policies of most film festivals but can't, in the final analysis, live without them.

In any case, the seasoned cinephile soon realises that many festivals' irreconcilable contradictions are the source of their appeal. Most of the major festivals are neither sites of unadulterated cinematic nirvana or mere hollow spectacles. A certain number – especially the most popular, and therefore most controversial, events such as Cannes and Toronto – combine both elements. Even the Venice Film Festival of the Mussolini era, an event that appears thoroughly corrupt and degraded to contemporary observers, screened a certain number of artistically worthy films untainted by fascist imperatives. And even the festivals most beloved by cinephiles for their integrity and altruism – Rotterdam and Vienna come easily to mind – frequently disappoint discerning critics, audiences and programmers. The delicate decisions, and myriad compromises, forced upon most film festival directors are discussed in the anthology's lively exchange between James Quandt, chief programmer at the Toronto Cinematheque and Simon Field, former director of the Rotterdam Film Festival and currently consultant to the Dubai International Film Festival. While certain cinephiles sneer at the efforts of large festivals to balance demanding arthouse fare with more crowd-pleasing films, Field defends what is termed the 'sandwich process' in the Netherlands – using 'bigger films to get audiences to support your festival and the smaller films'. This sort of savvy pragmatism is undoubtedly what fuels the success of many of the more notable festivals. The result is of course the phenomenon of the two-tiered festival: for example, large, primarily mainstream competitions at Cannes and Berlin counter-balanced by parallel events, the Directors' Fortnight and 'the Forum'. A more audience-oriented festival such as Rotterdam attempts to merge both the popular and the esoteric into one entity, albeit one that has considerably more space for experimental cinema than most mega-festivals. Nevertheless, Quandt, quite rightly, questions Field about film festivals' often-thorny roles as gatekeepers; a number of groundbreaking films and directors languish in obscurity because important festivals have proved timid about showcasing innovative, if 'difficult', work. It makes sense that many contributors to this volume are both critics and programmers; both Field and Quandt at least implicitly maintain that sagacious programming should be understood as a form of criticism (and analogous arguments are made in the essays by Rosenbaum, Koehler, Peranson, Quintín and Christoph Huber).

For most critics, programmers and the public, Cannes, for better or worse, has come to exemplify the quintessential film festival.[2] From the perspective of the international art cinema market (sales agents and distributors in tandem), Cannes' blessing functions as what, especially since the publication of Naomi Klein's *No Logo* (2002), has been critiqued as corporate 'branding'. As the film scholar Marijke de Valck observes in *Film Festivals: From European Geopolitics to Global Cinephilia*, 'The cultural value added by festival selection and programming reaches beyond the level of personal preference and becomes more or less – according to the festival's prestige on the international film circuit – globally acknowledged as evidence of quality. The process is similar to the way in which museums and art galleries add cultural capital to the artifacts they exhibit.'[3]

Quintín, like many commentators, grudgingly acknowledges that Cannes is the centre of 'the festival galaxy'. Just as Pascale Casanova maintains that 'Paris became the place where books – submitted to critical judgment and transmuted – can be denationalised and their authors made universal',[4] Cannes also retains enough of the French Enlightenment tradition to make an effort to 'universalise' (and, by implication, make safe for arthouse consumption) such disparate directors as Abbas Kiarostami, Michael Haneke and Béla Tarr. Although all of these directors have been honoured with films in the official Cannes competition, their canonisation has been, at least to a certain extent, the byproduct of the more experimental programming of *La Quinzaine de Réalisateurs*, or Directors' Fortnight – a sidebar inaugurated in 1969 as a response to criticism of Cannes' hidebound programming that came to the fore in May 1968 – when, as every cinephile knows, the spectacle was interrupted and a group of militant filmmakers shut down the glitz machine for a year. During the 2008 Directors' Fortnight, not coincidentally the fortieth anniversary of May '68, Olivier Jahan's documentary *40x15* chronicled the history of this prestigious 'parallel festival'. Jahan documents the affinities between the Fortnight's antinomian cinephilia and the spirit of '68, particularly as exemplified by Pierre-Henri Deleau, the director of the sidebar during its formative years. In one of the film's many trenchant interviews with former Quinzaine directors, Ken Loach maintains that the early decades of the Quinzaine nurtured a cherished pocket of 'subversion'. Jahan's film is peppered with similar fervent testimonials from directors ranging from American independents such as Jim Jarmusch to European cineastes such as Chantal Akerman and Werner Herzog.

The advent of the Quinzaine in the late 1960s also heralded the emergence of the idealistic programmer as de facto critic and this volume's case studies of disparate film festivals highlights both altruistic festivals where programmers aspire towards at least a quasi-utopian festival space free of commodification and dystopian events where crass commercialism, and even rampant corruption, reign supreme. Olaf Möller, who himself doubles as a programmer as well as a critic, celebrates two off-the-beaten-path festivals, Kino Otok in Slovenia and i 1000 occhi in northern Italy, that are exemplary for celebrating 'anarchistic freedom' and 'a sense of wonder'. By contrast, Kong Rithdee's article on the troubled history of the Bangkok International Film Festival examines a catastrophically mismanaged festival that failed miserably to serve the needs of the local community and its avid cinephiles. Of course, most festivals exist somewhere between these two polarities. While the Viennale is often cited for its adventurous programming, the Austrian critic Christoph Huber finds much to quibble about, as well as praise, while reminiscing about his years attending what is certainly one of the seminal events on the film festival calendar. Although film buffs might speak of festivals in terms of aesthetic epiphanies or disasters, even the smallest of them are essentially bureaucracies susceptible to the winds of critical favour and the unpredictability of market forces – something like stocks that are favoured one day and plunge the next. Stephen Teo's analysis of the shifting fortunes of the Pusan International Film Festival, the Singapore International Film Festival and the Hong Kong International Film Festival emphasises that the fate of festivals depend upon various institutional factors that are often beyond the organisers' control: changes in governmental policy, economic recession, and technological changes that inspire 'real concern over whether' these festivals 'can be attractive and relevant to newer, younger audiences and their environment of new digital technology and inter-digital media (IDM)'.

Most of the critics and programmers featured in this anthology flaunt their 'strong opinions' (to invoke Vladimir Nabokov's encomium) as badges of honour. While Atom Egoyan is no less opinionated, in the interview that concludes this volume he, perhaps inevitably (embodying someone who must traverse art and commerce on a regular basis), exemplifies a more pragmatic spirit. As a director whose career has been linked to the festival circuit since its inception, he has been on both sides of the fence – on the one hand, a seemingly rarefied director of art cinema who gradually followed the route to more mainstream acceptance as well as someone responsible for at least one straightforwardly commercial film. Yet Egoyan seems to have few doubts that his present success would have been practically unimaginable without the existence of certain key supportive film festivals. And, despite occasional annoyances and disappointments, Egoyan, like Jonathan Rosenbaum in his memoir, recalls the pleasures of festival discoveries and encounters with great vividness. After all is said and done, the search for pleasure, however fleeting or futile, is at the heart of the festival experience.

Given this publication's long lead time, it's inevitable that certain details will have changed, or are in flux, since the authors initially submitted their articles. For example, James Quandt and Simon's Field's misgivings concerning the confusing tangle of sections at the Rotterdam Film Festival were partially addressed in 2009 by director Rutger Wolfson's decision to streamline the myriad sections into three, easy-to remember rubrics. Yet, in the final analysis, Wolfson's overhaul was merely cosmetic and failed to make navigating Rotterdam much easier than in previous years. Other changes in the nature of festivals may go beyond mere bureaucratic finagling. As this edition of *Dekalog* goes to print, the euphemistically named 'economic downturn' is in full swing – financial turmoil that may well undercut the hegemony of the sales agents who wield power at international festivals and change the contours of the cutthroat marketplace machinations examined by Peranson in his well-reasoned polemic.

Several people have proved extremely supportive of this project since its inception. When I was in the planning stages, both Jonathan Rosenbaum and James Quandt provided encouragement and were very helpful in suggesting names of potential contributors. Adrian Martin was on target in suggesting the appropriateness of translating the Bazin essay and proved unfailingly enthusiastic when the translation materialised. It also goes without saying that I am indebted to the hard work and good cheer of translators Emilie Bickerton and Joan and Dennis West.

I am also grateful that my colleagues at *Cineaste*, Gary Crowdus and Cynthia Lucia, found this anthology of interest and agreed to publicise it by publishing Mark Peranson's article in our Summer 2008 issue. Marcy Gerstein was extremely helpful in facilitating a phone interview with Atom Egoyan, and Egoyan himself, despite a tight schedule, was wonderfully agreeable, and even proved unflappable when certain technical snafus interrupted our phone conversation. Finally, Yoram Allon of Wallflower Press, who gave me a contract for this *Dekalog* installment shortly after I suggested it, endured the various snags and delays that often accompany compiling anthologies with admirable aplomb.

NOTES

1   See Alessandro Falassi (ed.) (1987) *Time Out of Time: Essays on the Festival*. Albuquerque: University of New Mexico Press. In a lecture to the 10th International Women's Film Festival in Seoul, the Australian critic Meaghan Morris demarcates something she terms the 'festive principle': 'a political principle which manoeuvres between the harsh "reality principle" which institutions are dedicated to reproducing, and the "pleasure principle" which alone (I think) can over the historical long term sustain the "good" narcissism of collective self-love and shared self-respect that social movements must affirm if they are to flourish.' Thanks to Adrian Martin for calling my attention to this unpublished lecture.

2   For a useful history of Cannes, see Kieron Corless and Chris Darke (2007) *Cannes: Inside the World's Premier Film Festival*. London: Faber and Faber. For an analysis of the role of Cannes in the 'cultural history of the postwar era', see 'The Cannes Film Festival and the Marketing of Cosmopolitanism', in Vanessa R. Schwartz (2007) *It's So French: Hollywood, Paris, and the Making of Cosmopolitan Film Culture*. Chicago: The University of Chicago Press, 57–99.

3   Marijke de Valck (2008) *Film Festivals: From European Geopolitics to Global Cinephilia*. Amsterdam: Amsterdam University Press, 186–7.

4   Pascale Casanova (2004) *The World Republic of Letters*. Trans. M. B. DeBevoise. Cambridge, MA: Harvard University Press, 127. The last *Cahiers du cinéma* 'Atlas' issue of 2008 (a bilingual 'Special Issue' published 'hors série') includes a special issue entitled 'Film Festivals Worldwide' which constitutes a self-analysis from the French perspective of the importance of Cannes – particularly in a joint interview with Gilles Jacob and Thierry Frémaux, respectively the President and General Delegate of the Cannes festival – and also includes ruminations on Sundance and Il Cinema Ritrovato, 'the festival of restored films of the Bologna Cineteca'.

I.

A BACKWARD GLANCE

The Festival Viewed as a Religious Order

ANDRÉ BAZIN in *Cahiers du cinéma* (June 1955)

(Translated by Emilie Bickerton)

In 1955, when this short article appeared in Cahiers du cinéma, *37-year-old André Bazin was one of the most influential and respected film critics of his generation, with an international reputation as formidable as his domestic one. He is best known today for co-founding* Cahiers, *but his prolific writing on the medium appeared in a variety of magazines, newspapers and journals. His book* Qu'est ce que le cinéma? *remains one of the canonical works of film criticism; his (incomplete but published) biographies of Orson Welles and Jean Renoir are very original accounts of these directors' works. This legacy is even more formidable for the shortness of his life: he died three years after this article was published.*

Bazin had worked in cinema since the early 1940s, living through as well as heavily influencing the next two explosive decades in the medium. Although the film festival circuit was relatively newly established – Venice (1932), Cannes (founded 1939, launched in 1946), Locarno (1946), Berlin (1951), Rotterdam (1972) – and retained an independence from producers and the industry that no longer exists in today's hob-nobbing and glitz on the Croisette, the momentum was already moving in this direction. For Bazin these festivals were mostly humiliating spectacles, with

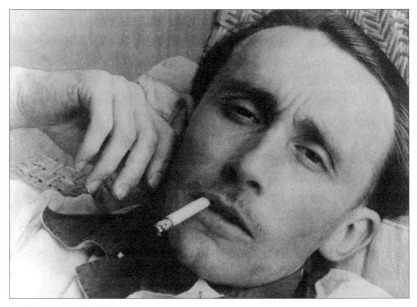

André Bazin (1918–1958)

cinema decking itself out as a whore for two weeks. He had founded his own 'anti-Cannes' in 1948 and 1949, with the 'Festival du Film Maudit'. In an earlier report Bazin had been far more direct in his condemnation of the pomp and ceremony that eclipsed the films being shown: 'Why can't we have a serious geology?' of the cinematic art, he asked in 1953, rather than the 'flashy geography' on display at Cannes.

A topic Bazin typically weaved into his writing was reference to the natural world. His passion for animals was evident privately – his home was full of them, from cats to iguanas, and even a crocodile in the bathtub – and intellectually, with his early influences including evolutionary theorist Teilhard de Chardin. Nature and cinema were treated in similar ways: 'He watched films as if they were animals temporarily captive', Dudley Andrew has explained, 'he gave to them the dignity of independent existence, yet he slipped himself inside that existence until, in his best moments, he approached the world of another conscience and was able to describe its structure and rules.'[1]

The peculiar structure, rituals and rules of film festivals, particularly Cannes as experienced by the journalists in attendance, is perfectly captured in this lucid essay. Festivals function as highly regulated retreats where critics and artists adhere to the rules strictly, obsessively — and ultimately — futilely. The trappings of religion characterise the film festival, Bazin noted, but the spiritual centre was absent; sincerity and belief were discarded like empty shells before the walk onto the red carpet. You had, in other words, the strangeness of devout religious observance, without God or faith. Bazin partly mocked this, and mostly mourned it.

— Emilie Bickerton
Assistant Editor, *New Left Review*

Viewed from the outside, a Festival, and in particular the one at Cannes, seems the very epitome of a worldly affair. But for what one might call the professional festivalgoer, namely the cinema critics, there is nothing that is more serious and also less 'worldly' (as Pascal would understand the word). Having 'done' almost all of them since 1946 I have witnessed first-hand the gradual perfecting of the Festival phenomenon, the practical creation of its *rituals* and its inevitable establishment of hierarchies. Its history is comparable, I would suggest, to the foundation of a religious Order; fully-fledged participation in the Festival is like being provisionally admitted to convent life. Indeed, the Palace which rises up on the Croisette is nothing less than the present-day monastery of the moviemaker.

Some may think that I'm trying to be paradoxical. Nothing is farther from the truth. This comparison struck me unprompted at the end of seventeen days of pious retreat and fully 'regulated' living. If an Order is something defined by its rules as well as being inseparable from a life of contemplation and meditation, in which people join in holy worship of a common transcendent reality, then the Festival is a religious Order. Film writers come together from all corners of the globe to spend two weeks living a life diametrically opposed to their everyday professional and private existence. In the first place they come as 'invitees', experiencing comfort but nevertheless a degree of austerity (the palaces are reserved for members of the jury, the stars and producers). Such a level of luxury is perfectly appropriate for the work they do, and I would swap many a monastic cell with which I am acquainted for a room at the S. Hotel or M. Hotel, apart from the wooden beds, of course! This being said, one member of the 1954 jury, Luis Buñuel, was not slow to have his mattress at the Carlton replaced by the wooden table he habitually sleeps upon.

The main feature of festival life lies in its moral obligations and the regularity of all its activities. Journalists are woken around 9.00 a.m. The daily ritual is brought up with the breakfast, in the shape of the two Festival newspapers, the bulletins from *Cinémato* and *Film Français*. These describe the day's offices. They are not called *Lauds*, *Matins* and *Vespers* but rather 'Dawn', 'Matinée' and 'Evening'. Just in the same way that the 'déjeuner' (literally 'breaking the fast') has become the second meal of the day and that the 'dîner' has moved, in the space of two hundred years, to replace 'supper', so the Festival's 'matinées' have become vesperal, and the 'evening' performances nocturnal. Whatever the lateness of the hour at which our Festivalgoer retires to bed, he's up in time for 'dawn', that is to say for the private screenings at 10.30 a.m. The service is held in one of the chapels in the town. One then returns to the Motherhouse for the *Cérémonie du casier*.[2] This consists of getting from the Press Office the day's articles, the press releases for the films being shown, and the invites that haven't been sent directly to the hotels. By now it is 12.30, and usually time for a press conference which will provide matters to reflect upon during a late lunch. At 3.00 we're on the go again for the afternoon film in the Palace basilica. Since the rites at Vespers are none too reliable I'll describe the evening procedures. You go out at 6.00. Reporters for the morning editions begin to ruminate on the piece they will phone in at eight o'clock. The others are more relaxed and head for cocktails at around 6.30. Dinner at 8.30 ushers in the day's most important ceremony: choice of habit. The Festival Order has strict dress code for evening services, at least. I am old enough to have been present when the rules were instituted and even to have been subjected to them. For the first Festivals in Cannes and Venice the rules were not yet binding. Journalism's young Turks, and to a lesser extent some from pre-war days with working-class affinities, looked down their noses at dinner jackets. Even a dark suit could cause them problems. But I saw them all give way, one by one. First there was the year when they begged or borrowed a friend's rather tight tux with its outdated lapels, but then they eventually succumbed and took their vows. Today the whole press corps wears the uniform, and it all seems perfectly normal. Personally, and I can admit to it without any false embarrassment, tuxedos look good on me, especially white ones, although the bow tie still has me in knots!

But clothes don't make the man, and membership in the Order is conferred by an electronic machine dispensing uncopiable cards, which will get you in. Once you're standing on holy ground another hierarchy rises up – what might be called functional discrimination. The press have reserved seats in the orchestra between rows 6 and 10. And if left to themselves that's exactly where their long experience would take them. They'll have nothing to do with the balcony, which is too far from the screen and just about right for members of the jury and the stars. Everyone's eyes are on the balcony, though. And it cannot be otherwise, since the design of the Palais is a challenge to the way people conduct themselves at the Festival. The rules require the show to take place in the auditorium, and to start even the moment people enter it. At Cannes the entrances are ridiculously narrow and lead to a terrible crush going in and out. In years when the weather is bad the trampling of guests in the rain sounds the death knell for evening gowns. At Venice they have understood the problem and built an enormous front canopy where people can spend as long as they want looking at each other. Cannes, on the other hand, disregarded the existence of open ground nearby in favour of jamming the Palais right up next to the Croisette, thereby rendering such idiocy permanent. As regards the interior, one must acknowledge a degree of harmony in the design and the colour scheme, but the position of the orchestra relative to the balcony denies paying spectators the very pleasure they have come in order to enjoy. A point which constantly enhances the sense of superiority felt by members of the press. With their blasé god-given eyeball-to-eyeball glances at Lollobrigida, journalists relish their distinction from the common horde who would do anything just to see their idol. We who know that religion needs such dramatic displays and gilded liturgy also know where to find the true God; if such demonstrations engender in us a sense of condescending or amused pity rather than the disgust that purifies, it is because we know that, when all is said and done, everything resounds to his greater glory.

At about half past midnight we find ourselves on the Croisette, and soon we are getting together in small groups in the nearby bars to discuss the day's films over a *citron pressé*. An hour later we head off to bed. At 9 o'clock there is a knock, and it is breakfast heralding the rites of the new day.

In addition to the programme I have described there are the parties. Normally there are three or four worth noting, two of which are important: the Trip to the Islands, with its spicy fish soup and traditional striptease by the starlet of the year standing on the rocks, and then the closing banquet. Additional items come in the form of receptions offered by Unifrance, Unitalia and sometimes the *Mexicaine* or the *Espagnole*. Each of these receptions gives rise to little Kafkaesque dramas since part of the press corps is inexplicably overlooked. Those chosen feign indignant compassion and join with those forgotten in railing against the poor quality of an organisation which can alone be responsible for such a clumsy oversight. Secretly, however, they are proud at being amongst the chosen, this time at least. A prime example occurred in the first year with the unforgettable Soviet reception where invitations were clearly pulled out of a hat. *Le Figaro* made it whereas Sadoul was left out. You can just imagine the politico-diplomatic interpretations that ran all afternoon.

Whilst from a liturgical standpoint the most important celebration is the Flower Fight which takes place halfway through the Festival, this largely represents an opportunity for the critics to relax for an afternoon and escape. This is because it marks a definite change to the daily rituals. Until then the pace of screenings and festivities has been relatively tranquil. Halfway through it suddenly accelerates. Private showings start about then, and most people with only five days or a week to spare for the Festival turn up for the second half in the knowledge that it is the most lively part. From this point on the daily ordeal is unrelenting and it is at this time above all that journalists live a monastic existence.

Some 15 or 18 days of such a regimen are enough to disorientate a Parisian critic, I can tell you. When he gets back to his home and everyday working life he feels as though he's come back from far away, having spent a long spell in a world where order, rigour and necessity reign. It is more redolent by far of an amazing albeit hard-working retreat, with cinema as its unifying spiritual focus, than of the experience of a lucky winner of admittance to a giant orgy, echoes of which he might find with incredulity in the pages of *Cinémonde* or *Paris Match*.

NOTES

1 Dudley Andrew (1978), *André Bazin*. New York and Oxford: Oxford University Press, 12.

2 This is an allusion to the journalists' routine of checking their 'casier' or mailboxes. Once an act that required a personal key bequeathed to each critic at the start of the festival that would be used daily to retrieve the information about every forthcoming event, screening, interview, party. It was so integral to the experience of the festival that Bazin felt it took on the attributes of a ceremonial ritual.

II.

FILM FESTIVALS: BETWEEN ART AND COMMERCE

First You Get the Power, Then You Get the Money: Two Models of Film Festivals

MARK PERANSON

We've yet to reach the point, as rather trenchantly proposed by Mike Judge in the visionary satire *Idiocracy*, where the collective film experience consists of sitting in a common space and watching a film called *Ass*. Thanks, some would argue, to the role that film festivals play in our culture. It's true that film festivals in the current political economy of cinema exist as an alternative distribution network; their most significant purpose is providing audiences with opportunities to enjoy commercially unviable films projected in a communal space – films that most communities, even the most cosmopolitan, otherwise would not have the opportunity to see. Moreover, these festivals are popping up like Starbucks franchises, in terms of numbers – every major city now has one – and in terms of the products that they offer. The major festivals introduce trendy new sidebars on an annual basis, showing more and more films, and expanding to include, for example, art installations. Yet they still provide a venue for lively interplay between filmmaker and audience, or between film professionals. Festivals, it must be said and not forgotten – though it might seem like I'm doing so over the course of this analysis – create the general atmosphere for the appreciation of film as art, and, in our transitional time, are thus essential.

But this does not mean that the situation is perfect. There's a false dichotomy that exists between the multiplex and the film festival world, where one is business, the other art. If anything, one can say that in their local contexts, international film festivals are *too* successful, as the real spectre haunting the film world is declining attendances at so-called arthouse theatres year round, *especially* in screening facilities that are being built and run by film festivals. To state just one example of many, the North American premiere of Straub-Huillet's *Quei Loro Incontri* at the Cinematheque Ontario in Toronto, home to arguably the world's most successful film festival, drew a meagre audience of twenty or so people, albeit on a cold winter's night. Audiences surely are more willing to take chances during film festivals, a factor of the system of passes and, also, economics: ticket prices at film festivals, even not taking into account passes, are usually lower than at regular screenings (though not in Toronto, where they go for twenty bucks a pop!).

Festivals have a number of advantages over regular arthouse screenings, in that festivals are *events*. And we are currently living in an event-driven culture (as opposed to, say, a quality-driven culture). Because they are events (if not spectacles, in the Debordian sense), festivals have a greater promotional budget to attract audiences (especially special interest audiences, like local immigrant communities), they can market themselves as a focal event in the city, and locals (as well as tourists) take vacations around the time of festivals. Film festivals are not exclusively for cinephiles – they provide the opportunity for binging, so why should we be surprised when the attendance lags during the rest of the year. Not to mention that regular screenings of arthouse films find themselves competing with other film 'events' – documentary festivals, Asian festivals, queer festivals, children's festivals, mental health festivals, green film festivals, you name it. Just as many kinds of festivals, one could say, as choices of coffee at Starbucks, with just as much marketing involved.

Yet the best thing about film festivals is that they provide the opportunity for audiences to see films that, otherwise, they cannot see. Although content, or even aesthetic criteria, should be left out of this kind of discussion, inevitably it finds a way in through the back door. So why not let it in?

For argument's sake, let's say there are fifty outstanding films per year, films that any programmer or critic, personal taste aside, would agree are films that any self-respecting international film festival should show – works that will stand the test of time, or take the pulse of the time, *Ass* excluded. The expansion in the number of festivals worldwide, the busy calendar, especially in the fall, and the type of system that has organically developed over the past decade or so, restricts where these fifty films will play. Most of the time there is only one English-subtitled print of a film in the world – a film can only be in one place at one time, and, for reasons elucidated below, sales agents and/or producers often only want certain films to play in one festival per territory. Moreover, there exists a common preconception that an international film festival's priority is to show the very best of the year's output in world cinema/arthouse cinema (to be, as the Toronto International Film Festival used to be called, a 'Festival of Festivals'). But it's quite possible that no one festival is able to fulfil this lofty, yet quite achievable, goal, and that, indeed, it's nigh impossible for most festivals to even have this as a goal.

Two ideal festival models

Festivals here are seen as political actors, and by this I mean they are subjected to pressures from interest groups and that festivals exist in relation to each other, and, one could even argue, are in a constant struggle for power. In the course of this struggle, relationships of exploitation have come into place, where two kinds of film festivals coexist in an essentially core/periphery relationship. And the way it works may be ass-backwards: first you get the power, it seems, *then* you get the money.

These two *ideal* models encompass, on the one hand, characteristics typical to the operation of the film festival itself and, on the other, interest groups that must be appeased for the continuing support and success of the festival – and these interest groups influence what films and what *kinds* of films are going to be screened at a festival; the two charts (on pages 27 and 28) kind of relate to each other dialectically, as change in one leads to change in the other.

First, how can we characterise these two models, one I will call the 'business model' or, depending on my mood, the 'behemoth', the other being the 'audience model?' These models are ideal, but derived from my experience of both going to film festivals and working at film festivals. In particular, my viewpoint is coloured by working for the Vancouver International Film Festival, which likely slants this non-neutral information and breakdown in a specific way, though there's no sour grapes in this analysis: in fact, each kind of festival is subject to different kinds of external pressures.

For the benefit of people who might not have heard about Vancouver, let me detail some basic facts: the festival shows about 220 features each year to an audience of about 150,000 people, making it the second largest in North America. Besides screening the most Canadian features of any festival, there is also one of the largest East Asian programmes outside of Asia within an international festival (about forty programmes of Asian features and shorts a year). This includes a competition for first- or second-time filmmakers (past winners include Lee Chang-dong, Hong Sang-soo, Jia Zhangke and Koreeda Hirokazu). One of the niche goals that the festival established a while back was to serve as a kind of conduit to East Asia – for a lot of directors, coming to the festival marks the first time they've travelled outside of Asia, or their home countries. Yet despite these not insignificant accomplishments, I gather that most non-Canadians only have one Canadian film festival in their minds.

Examples of the business festival, then, would be major festivals with markets or de facto markets (Cannes, Berlin, Venice, Toronto, Pusan), plus, to a lesser extent, the largest festival in a country, while examples of audience festivals would be the greater number of the world's festivals, the one in a city near you (I could say Vancouver, but I could also say anything from Seattle to San Francisco to Vienna to Buenos Aires to any number of festivals under discussion in this volume). Once again, these are ideals: most festivals fit somewhere in the middle, combining elements of both types. It's also the case that festivals can move from one column to the other, typically the second to the first (for example, one could argue that Tribeca, buttressed by the support of American Express, is trying to do this, and that Pusan did this extremely quickly, creating both a film fund and a market while barely having enough time to grow facial hair).

BUSINESS FESTIVAL	AUDIENCE FESTIVAL
High budget, operating revenue not primarily audience/ticket sales	Low budget, a good deal of operating revenue comes from attendance
Premiere oriented (world or international)	Not concerned with premieres
Major corporate sponsorship	Limited corporate sponsorship
Guests present for most films	Limited number of guests
Market/business presence	Little business presence
Large staff	Small staff
Major competition	Minor competition
Film-fund/third-world investment	No investment in films
Retrospectives	Few retrospectives
Most films are submitted	Most films are seen at other festivals or solicited
Hollywood studio involvement	Little Hollywood studio involvement
Always expanding	Content to remain the same size

Chart 1. Two models for understanding film festivals

The second chart, overleaf, lists the separate groups that each have a vested interest in some part of the operations of the film festival, which influence what films screen at what festival – both what kind of films, and what films precisely, as far as things like premiere status is concerned; note that the interest groups are all interrelated, as when you are appeasing one, you're ill-treating another, so it's impossible to look at them in isolation. I've also numbered them in ideal importance, so that the distributor would be the first most important interest group in the business festival, and fourth in the audience festival (in this schematic).

INTEREST GROUP	BUSINESS FESTIVAL	AUDIENCE FESTIVAL
Distributor/ Buyer	1. Domestically, use as launching pad for soon-to-be-released films, take advantage of festival/presence of talent to hold press junkets; buyers attend festivals looking to acquire new films (leading to the need for a premiere-heavy lineup)	4. If distributor believes in good word of mouth creating audience, use to launch newer releases; buyer may attend to acquire in specialty areas (i.e. if festival is strong in documentaries, particular national cinemas ...)
Sales agent	2. A place to promote and sell films to distributors	5. Used as a revenue stream to fund their presence at business festivals
Sponsors	3. Need to be appeased, often with presence of celebrities	2. Need to be appeased, with 'sponsor films', more commercial films with stars or audience friendly
Government	4. Promotion of national cinema	3. Promotion of national cinema
Audience	5. Lesser concern, belief is they will see anything that has been branded by the festival and not complain	1. Major concern, but also underlying truth that tastes often vary from programmer to general public
Critics	6. Junkets for mainstream critics, 'artier' films for special press	6. Need to concern themselves with local critics' reactions as they are promotional tools for selling tickets
Filmmakers	7. Attend because of work, a chore, do major publicity	7. Not as much work (more like vacation), engage with audience, meet other filmmakers. Often younger filmmakers.

Chart 2. Interest groups and their importance at film festivals

Taking all of this into account, it's easy to see why even the biggest festivals don't show those fifty films: because the furthest consideration from most of these interest groups' collective minds is aesthetic accomplishment. Sponsors, for example, require films that will be entertaining and not marred by annoying subtitles; major distributors want to acquire, or promote, films that will be box-office draws; the government entities want to promote their national cinemas, and God knows how many out of thirty Canadian features will be in the top fifty films of the year. The hope still exists in major cities that the missing ones of the mythical fifty will return as theatrical releases or receive limited engagements in a cinematheque or art theatre – one recent advancement from the Cinematheque Ontario is a series called 'Toronto Premieres', which essentially means 'great films that were "rejected" by the Toronto film festival' – but using that terminology ('rejection') doesn't quite explain why they didn't show up. Yet few institutions can even afford to put together such a series because, for the most part, if you're dealing with sales agents, you're going to pay through the nose. (And as long as twenty people are coming to see a Straub-Huillet film that costs all those Euros to show, that series will be short-lived).

Who the hell are sales agents, and why should you care?

Most of the actors in the charts above are well-known, and the type of influence and the reason they exert it self-explanatory, but there might be one protagonist that the general public doesn't recognise, the actor who holds the most cards in the system as it currently exists. Perhaps the defining actor in the current political economy of the film festival is the sales agent, an entity that didn't exist a few decades ago. Sales agents arose because the festival distribution system required them. As film festivals are concerned, sales agents – whose main purpose exists to sell films for domestic distribution either theatrically or on video or DVD (or, increasingly, for direct download) – have come to serve the function of government agencies; for example, Unifrance used to be the entity that film festivals would deal with if they wanted to show French films – now by and large it's the sales agents (this example is pertinent as most of the powerful sales agents are in fact French). Meanwhile, Unifrance continues to exist, but has concentrated its efforts on the business festivals, or holding particular events to sell French films to distributors. This is not to say that government agencies have disappeared; their role has changed to that of promoter or facilitator. Telefilm Canada, which both funds and promotes Canadian films, is a key supporter of the large Canadian film festivals in terms of contributing to their budgets and, in exchange, the festivals (including Toronto and Vancouver), feature nationalistic showcases for the year's homegrown output. In addition, at many festivals worldwide they have a significant presence as a promotional entity – most significantly, for good reason, at the business festivals.

The big sales agents – Wild Bunch, Fortissimo, Celluloid Dreams (a.k.a. 'The Director's Label'), Films Distribution, Pyramide, Bavaria-Film – control the art film market, often investing in the films at production stage. They decide which festivals a film will play at, and often demand fees from festivals to cover 'their costs', costs that include participation at business festivals who generally aren't required to pay these screening fees. In other words, in a system with these rules, it's not a question of what films a festival 'can get', as if by dint of the programmers' sheer will-power, programming acumen, stamina, bribery or whatever, the films will appear in the line-up. It's better to see the deck as stacked the other way – the sales agents and distributors decide what films will play where. (And, for some reason, some sales agents decide to give coveted films to many festivals; in truth, it's a crapshoot how this plays out in reality.)

In this system, then, where a film plays is a question of power (or perceived power) as much as a question of money; so, for example, Toronto, which has both power and money, does not pay screening fees, and can essentially have its pick of whatever films they want – you'd think that they could pretty much show the fifty films and still have plenty of room left over for films that are meant to appease the other interest groups (such as middling gala films with celebrities for sponsors, challenging art films for snooty film critics and cinephiles, and so on). The reason, however, why they don't, is as much aligned with the need to appease other actors as it is to mere questions of taste, and the need to have world premieres (rather than, say, films that debuted earlier in the year way back in Berlin). Smaller festivals with less money are encouraged to screen 'older' films, films of arguably less artistic merit, and are expected to pay through the nose for them – the standard request these days is €1,000 for two screenings of a film. Essentially there seems to be a kind of a core/periphery system of exploitation, where the ever-increasing screening fees are becoming more and more essential to keep the system afloat. Yes, the larger festivals have more guests, and that is an expense, but this is a system that also allows for the sales agents to make fancy press booklets for Berlin, Cannes or Venice and throw lavish parties at those festivals (though a lot of that cost is passed back onto the producer).

In this economy, the term 'audience' only matters to a sales agent as a negative: meaning, the more people have seen the film in a territory, the less they can charge to a potential distributor. (Some distributors also have this policy – the alternative argument when it comes to distributors has to do with festivals generating good word of mouth). So, it's often the case that in smaller countries (including Canada, with a population of only thirty million), it's becoming more and more common to have a film screen only at festivals, even if those films possess arguably little commercial potential.

By keeping these factors in mind, one could confidently predict a good percentage of the competitions at the major European film festivals – as well as the bulk of the programmes at other festivals. If someone would ask me how to get a film into Cannes, Berlin, Venice or Toronto, I'd immediately recommend getting a powerful sales agent. An interesting read is always found in the Cannes opening press conference release, where (currently) Thierry Frémaux talks about some of the common themes offered up by the films, regional representation, old auteurs vs. newcomers, and so on – in essence, what you'd get as an introduction in your standard festival report, which should say something about who standard festival reports serve – but what is never mentioned in that release is likely the most important: who represents what films. Yes, there are French distributors to consider, though it is true that a lot of the films are picked up after being selected for competition (perhaps my French friends can enlighten me on this issue). But the key thing to look at is who is selling the film: in 2006, an amazing seven out of twenty titles were represented by Wild Bunch, a company that describes itself as 'dedicated to the nurture, development and creative exploitation of the radical, the innovative, the visionary, the truly extraordinary, in cinema world wide. Our only criteria are excellence, singularity of vision and that each new project offers a new challenge, a new development. Often controversial, always provocative, our line-up stands as our statement of intent.' The head of Wild Bunch, Vincent Maraval, goes so far as to say he is in consultation with Frémaux, as well as Venice's Marco Müller, throughout the year.

Within such a system, the best way for festivals to work to attract the films that they want is with, no doubt, cold hard cash. Over the past few years smaller festivals have started upping the prize money for their competitions; besides the ludicrous goings-on in Rome, where, in its first year, tens of thousands of Euros went to a film selected by an 'audience jury' – hell, you might as well just draw a name out of a hat. At the Gijon Film Festival in northern Spain, where I did some jury duty in 2006, I was vexed but not astonished to hear that the €25,000 prize went not to the filmmaker, but the sales agent or, if there was one, the local distributor (presumably to help promote the film upon its eventual release … yeah, right). In other words – and I know this for a fact – there are clear-cut cases where promises and assurances are made that to get more accomplished films from well-known auteurs, a slot in competition was promised, which in turn creates a situation of imbalance, as most of the films in similar competitions are from younger filmmakers, first or second films, and so forth. (In the Gijon case, it was Tsai Ming-liang's *I Don't Want to Sleep Alone*; a wise jury will recognise the film that's the odd duck and adjudicate accordingly.)

Is this a good idea or a bad idea? Intuitively, it's difficult not to conclude that this hurts both the festivals and the filmmakers, who receive little benefit from these screenings, save the occasional business trip. Shouldn't the filmmakers be the ones who reap the benefits as they actually make the films, and organise themselves in collectives (such as is often done in the world of experimental film, for example)? And as it is, when the films are sold internationally by sales agents, filmmakers – and even sales agents – make little money. (It's hard to extract solid numbers on how much a sales agent makes from the sale of a small arthouse film: I asked a Canadian distributor for numbers on various films and they said they sign confidentiality agreements about their deals). On the other hand, in a world with so many film festivals, who else is going to be responsible for organising the screenings, print shipping and other logistics? It's not an easy and simple job: there, I've even said something nice about sales agents. Despite all their power, I certainly don't envy them, and I wouldn't want to be one.

The ever-expanding film festival: notes from Berlin and Sundance

One significant conclusion that follows from a clear-eyed assessment of the current system is that many festivals are in fact ill-equipped to handle the change that's happening in the world because they are either resistant to change or if they do change – and many, as I said, are expanding – the drive for change comes either from within or in response to another festival's expansion. In other words, not from actual changes in the way films are made and being distributed (a massive topic better left for another time, but suffice to say I'm talking here about the Internet, video on demand and the decline of traditional cinema/arthouse filmgoing).

Premiere-heavy festivals such as Berlin and Sundance do just as much harm as good to the world of cinema. Most obviously, this harm results from nurturing a specific kind of festival film, one with potential crossover success. The major festivals always feature numerous examples of films attempting to replicate the success of more talented precursors. The more egregious of the recent crop of Sundance *Rushmore* clones, Jeffrey Blitz's *Rocket Science*, is watchable and amusing, but one would expect nothing less from a dramedy set in the cutthroat world of high-school debating. But even on paper its premise – that a preternaturally shy protagonist burdened by a hefty speech impediment would become a debater out of a misguided attraction to a conniving bitch – is simply ludicrous, and the paint-by-Anderson screenplay doesn't help. More poignant – perhaps because of the added points for being British and focusing on younger kids, who by nature are cuter – Hammer and Tongs' *Son of Rambow* mined the same vein and hit a rich ore of filmic references, adolescent friendship and, in a tolerable fashion, French-baiting.

Such feeble attempts at what's known in the biz as a 'Sundance film' – often involving emotionally damaged characters, and featuring costume design as character shorthand (ugly glasses='retard', especially on Dylan Baker), as exemplified by Ryan Eslinger's turkey, *When a Man Falls in a Forest* – are no longer the exclusive territory of the Lab that developed it: Eslinger's Sharon Stone-starring film premiered in the star-heavy Berlin competition, and will go down in history only for its press kit, clearly written by Stone or a representative. Speaking of French-baiting, Berlin saw the premiere of

Son of Rambow, an audience favourite, premiered at the 2007 Sundance Festival

the inexplicably popular Sundancey *2 Days in Paris*, a delusional rant from Julie Delpy's subconscious, which took pleasure in portraying the French as, depending on the moment, racist, sexist, delinquent, obnoxious and, in general, a lower life-form (Delpy's parents in particular). Back at Sundance, its mirror image, Zoe Cassavetes' Parker Posey-starring *Broken English*, still left Xan as the most talented of the siblings. The two festivals are becoming more similar than either would admit, thanks to a similar cross-colonisation: the larger a festival gets, the more weakly it is able to define its own space.

So change they must. Both Berlin and Sundance, like many of the behemoth festivals, have attempted in recent years to change the way they present themselves. Sundance's first, and most successful historical move, was to nurture the documentary through its Documentary Film Fund. Though the most impressive features in 2007 came from outside, with two cinematic Documentary Competition stand-outs *Zoo* and *Manda Bala (Send a Bullet)*, the general agreement is that the Sundance documentary crop continues to impress. Then the Sundance powers came up with the World Cinema Competition, featuring a number of forgettable films that turned up as cannon fodder in Berlin sidebars, which can be interpreted as a strategy to attract foreign sales agents in a market-less environment, as if there really need to be more people in Park City. In 2007 Sundance felt impelled to expand its 'alternative' programming – the same alternative strand that spawned the non-experimental *Old Joy* – just like the Berlin Forum 'Expanded' last year to include art installations, pandering, as my argument goes, to the artier critics, but also giving another bone to a festival sponsor (in this case, Sony): the Frontier has spawned the dimly-lit installation bunker New Frontier (one eagerly awaits the 'Final Frontier'), and Park City, if not the world, will never be the same. (In 2008 Sundance announced the brand-new 'Creative Producing Initiative, and the world will still never be the same.)

With these moves, Sundance is attempting to move from being a showcase for American independent films to being another one of the festival behemoths, like Berlin, Cannes or Toronto, which in 2007 added its own shoddy programme of art installations. These behemoths are driven internally by a constant need to expand, whether or not it's necessary, creating a spiral of escalation reminiscent of the Cold War arms race, but rarely in response to the realities of a changing film world. Does any film festival *really* require, like Berlin, a 'Talent Campus?' Why the sudden interest in colonising the Third World through world cinema funds which, though certainly valuable, often end up influencing the kind of film that is made?

Film critics and change

Besides whoring him or herself out, how does a film critic respond when faced with such a mindboggling number of options to choose from, in such a short time? (Many critics only attend such festivals for less than the full time, and also have to make time to consume mass quantities of alcohol in the evenings to forget the atrocities foisted upon them earlier that day). In reports, one often sees the comment that a festival is 'many festivals in one', and that each critic 'makes his/her own festival'. These 'many festivals' act in concert, the more obscure sidebars serving the more art-demanding critics and audiences, the more openly commercial elements – often in the form of the competition – serving the daily critics, the sponsors, the sales agents, and that amorphous entity known as 'the audience'. And there are only so many hours in a day, so many days in a festival. A competition becomes a kind of 'mini-festival' selected by the programmers to guide critics to write their 'think pieces', and to appeal to those viewers who would rather not be confronted with the possibility of choice and the probability of originality. In the final analysis, a competition mainly serves other interest groups such as sales agents, distributors and the all-important big money sponsors, who love the presence of celebrities (especially, it would seem, in Berlin).

Over the past few years, something strange is happening: some critics are actually noticing the poor quality of major competitions, or big premieres at non-competitive festivals (like Toronto). Yet the lowest common denominator approach of most competitions is being noticed by critics who have (a) seen times when being 'in competition' meant something and (b) are daring enough to actually venture towards the better films that find their homes in sidebars like the Directors' Fortnight in Cannes. Of course, film critics have also been conditioned by this power system to minimise the aesthetic contributions of audience festivals, concentrating whatever power they have on the larger business festivals, to the point of printing plainly inaccurate information because they care more about impressing the media offices of the business festivals than reporting actual information (or, if you prefer, helping out the little guy).

While the behemoth festivals may be sowing their own seeds of discontent, it will take more than a few critics screaming in the wilderness for revolution to happen. Until the system ceases to function for those more powerful interest groups, I can't see change happening. Change will occur when those people think that change is necessary, and, for the most part – the top rung of the ladder as it were – that will be when those groups (distributors, sales agents, sponsors) aren't making money, or see that film festivals are no longer serving their needs/interests. That time might be near, as today it's possible that by the year's end one could conceivably download (or have someone send you via a file transfer system) most of those mythical fifty films, whether or not they have distribution, important sales agents or widespread festival participation (or buy them legally from other countries over the internet, if one wanted to remain above board).

In the current configuration, critics can serve an important purpose by helping people (and other critics who might not know better) understand how the system operates, by doing something different rather than the typical journalistic festival piece that we all know, write and love – that the combination of anecdotal generalities, travel report and the occasional summation of a stand-out film in, at most, one or two paragraphs. There is another option, though, that doesn't involve selling your soul, and that has to do with inventive retrospectives, the type that places like, say, Vienna and (pre-Moretti) Torino have made a habit of doing, that gives critics something unique to write about that doesn't involve the unhealthy focus on premieres. I would discourage value judgement about festivals by and large, but if you wanted to assess a festival, perhaps you should look at what they don't show as much as what they do show. (And, as I've already noted, change the language: for example, instead of 'couldn't get' a certain film, say 'weren't given'.) Or compare festivals in each of the categories, but not across categories. Essentially, each festival should be treated on its own strengths, and with knowledge of the limits that it's under. It's not enough to look at a major festival's competition and say 'this was an off year' – the real criticism that should be made is of the system itself. All of this, combined, is what I hope I've accomplished here, as well as providing many avenues for future attack. As even if a film festival managed, by some combination of luck, smarts and circumstance, to find those fifty films and bring them to a local audience, the problems that I've outlined won't go away, and to think anything else would be delusional.

The Festival Galaxy

QUINTÍN

(Translated by Dennis West and Joan M. West)

1. A Brave New World

For three years now, I've been living in San Clemente, a little town on the
Argentine coast. When I was a kid, in the 1950s and 1960s, I used to spend
my vacations here. There were two movie houses and then, for a time,
three. As a teenager, I frequented them daily during the summertime. I saw
all kinds of pictures there – principally Hollywood movies – as double features: there were westerns, comedies, crime flicks; but there were also European films. Without even knowing who the directors were, I saw films by
John Ford, Jerry Lewis (enormously popular back then), Orson Welles, but
also Eric Rohmer, Jacques Tati and even Ingmar Bergman (when I managed to avoid age restrictions). I remember my most impressive afternoon
at the movies, a Fritz Lang double-bill – *The Indian Tomb* and *The Tiger of
Eschnapur*. Those theatres were not repertory or arthouses.

Nowadays there are still two movie houses in town, although one is seldom used. This is an extraordinary privilege for a city of 10,000 inhabitants
anywhere in the world. But San Clemente is still a vacation spot. The movie
theatre is open from January to March and certain weekends in the winter.
Up and down the coast there are other similar towns, with some ten movie
houses in total. They all belong to the same owner. And the movies he shows
– that are passed on from one movie house to the next – are the big blockbusters, especially the ones aimed at children. The films exhibited during

Quintín (Eduardo Antín), former director of BAFICI

summer do not number more than fifteen, as opposed to the 150 per season that were shown when I was a kid. These days, I subscribe to the most sophisticated cable/satellite system available in Argentina; and I have purchased all the film packages that are offered: the selection now available is only ten per cent of what used to be seen on pre-cable television in the 1960s. As for the town's video rental store, it is so bad that it only offers pirated DVD and tape copies; and the selection of titles is sparse and poor.

Everybody knows the story that I've just told, but it really only made sense to me when I moved to San Clemente after having lived my whole life in Buenos Aires, a big capital city. The title of this story should be: *Of How Cinema – A Cinema More or Less Copious, More or Less Diverse – Became Inaccessible for the Everyday Spectator Around the World.* It is true that now, even in my town, there are individuals downloading movies off the internet – and on the streets pirated DVDs are sold. But such practices are not part of the experience of the average citizen. This state of affairs started to become definitive around 1995, when the multiplexes were taking the place of the old movie houses and when most cities were being left without a movie theatre. It was around that time that film festivals started to grow and multiply. There is an evident correlation between these phenomena. Nowadays, the programme of a mid-sized festival (let's say, about 200 films) is equivalent to what one used to be able to see throughout the year in first-run cinemas – excluding Hollywood pictures. Or at least that was the situation in countries, such as Argentina, where there was wide distribution. Given these changes in the exhibition and distribution sectors – including the issue of where the audience now goes to see non-mainstream movies – the question is not whether a city has movie houses, but whether it hosts a good film festival. (Of course, the great majority of cities do not have film festivals.) If one charts the points on a planisphere, the difference is apparent. In the old days, the map of cinema was a variegated swarm of points occupying the inhabited part of the planet. Nowadays the new map, the festival one, is a sparse aggregate in which each element is perfectly distinguishable. The interesting thing, however, is that those isolated points constitute an organic network, a significant system. A galaxy. This is where present-day cinema finds its expression, even though another galaxy – the one made up of every home and every computer – also defines the present (and the future), albeit in another sense.

Fifty years ago film festivals already existed. But, at that time, they were few and irrelevant in terms of film commerce apart from their contribution to publicity and glamour. Rather than forming a system, they were a collection of eccentricities. Festivals were born as an effort by European states to appropriate the life of the movies: like a world fair or the Olympics, festivals were conceived of as an opportunity to show off the power, real or symbolic, of the host country as opposed to that of other countries. It's not by chance that the first important film festival, Venice, was created by Mussolini; nor was it by chance that Cannes was invented to counterbalance it. Nor that here, only a hundred miles from my town, Perón founded the Festival of Mar del Plata in 1954.

It's curious that it's only in the last few years that the Americans have established a major film festival such as Sundance. Since Hollywood was officially separated from the state, very early on it sketched out its own constellation on the world map. Over the years, the Hollywood circuit has become more and more digital (and even virtual); and movie-houses have become less important in the grand scheme of things. Now, non-Hollywood cinema no longer shares any physical space with the studios; rather, it circulates on its own highways.

The film festival constellation underwent a notable change in the past decade. Several stars burst out of a black hole, such as Pusan which was founded in 1996 and nowadays is the biggest of the Asian festivals. Other festivals have expanded exponentially – Toronto, for example, not long ago a small independent event and today a giant. Even though several stars have lost some of their lustre, the decade was marked by multiple births and by general growth. Two years ago, as the movie world marvelled at a multi-million dollar festival in Dubai, a yet-bigger multi-million dollar festival was already being created in the nearby Emirate of Abu Dhabi. Throughout Europe, throughout Latin America, throughout Asia, there are few mayors who can resist the temptation to create a film festival in her/his city. Rome is the most impressive example – an event inconceivable not long ago that attempts to surpass Venice in terms of glamour and to promote the political ascent of the *signore sindaco*. In Argentina around 1990, there was no film festival. Nowadays, there are more than twenty, including two major events: a re-born Mar del Plata and the 'independent' Festival of Buenos Aires (BAFICI), currently, perhaps the most important festival on the continent. BAFICI was only created in 1999, but it has already inspired responses in Santiago de Chile and Mexico City, and even in Lisbon.

Even before film festivals started sprouting up – like mushrooms after a good rain – there had been an attempt to organise them, to halt the chaos, and to impose order on the young galaxy. It was a rather bureaucratic organisational scheme, Stalinist in effect, and one that signalled the transformation of state-run festivals into industry festivals. FIAPF, an international federation of producers, established hierarchies, rules and legitimacy requirements for festivals as well as systems for circulating films amongst them. Thus 'Category A' festivals were born. While no one ever knew what a Category B or Category C festival was, the Category A festivals were dedicated to assembling competitive sections that boasted international premieres of the most outstanding films. As the years went by, the result was curious. The three truly big festivals – Cannes, Venice and Berlin – became even bigger while the second-tier festivals shrank. These second-tier Category A festivals – Karlovy Vary, San Sebastián, Moscow, Cairo, Mar del Plata, Montreal, Tokyo – all became less relevant because of one fundamental reason: there are not enough films to premiere in order to fulfill expectations, since the producers all attempt to get their films into Cannes first and secondly into Venice or Berlin. Beyond the first tier, producers don't really care about A festivals, or, more precisely, they prefer opening elsewhere. The Category A festivals are the falling stars of the galaxy – they are dull, fading, provincial caricatures of the old red-carpet routines.

Another type of festival has also fallen into decline after having reached its zenith: the big regional event. Havana offers a notable example: formerly a Mecca for Latin American cinema, it is today a holdover state-run festival and a permanent reminder that the island remains under the control of a dictator. Or there is the case of the Ouagadougou Festival in Burkina Faso, a reminder of a time when the dream of a significant, abundant and exportable African film industry still existed. Then too, the culture of the pompous film festival, the festival overloaded with stars and bureaucrats continues in Guadalajara, in Shanghai, in Vladivostok, and in the many provincial events around the world in which the press and the authorities – usually the festival's partial or full sponsors – cannot stand the idea of not having a figure of worldwide renown at the opening ceremonies. And, combined with other more contemporary formats, there still exists the *Cinéma du Monde* concept, of which Montreal continues to offer a perfect example. In this kind of festival, films from all countries are shown – generally bad, 'official' films – which represent a given country's typical industrial output and which exemplify the greater portion of worldwide production.

Still, even the most mediocre or worst programmed festivals do not lack audiences. The reason is very simple: they show what cannot be seen elsewhere. This happens for two reasons. One is that, in effect, there are films that only circulate in the Galaxy of the Festivals. But it also happens with increasing frequency that the same film which causes a sensation in a festival often is not at all successful when it opens commercially, or when it is shown in a cinémathèque, or in a repertory house. This tends to happen because festivals, since they belong to an 'event culture', to a culture of the extraordinary, end up being more significant as social acts than for their content. Furthermore, festivals do not merely disseminate a sizable portion of films produced each year; they also monopolise it. Therefore, the Galaxy becomes more and more substantial but more and more exclusive.

The proof of this dynamic is the following fact: film distribution is disappearing. International sales agents used to consider the festivals as beachheads in their efforts to sell film rights. Today those agents know that only happens in a few festivals: Cannes and Toronto, for example, and maybe Venice and Berlin. But this is generally not the case: the exhibition of a film at Pusan does not guarantee the film's premiere in Korea, nor does playing at Rotterdam insure a premiere in Holland. Films are purchased in the great markets, and the reception by audiences in the festivals themselves is not so important for buying purposes. Since motion pictures are no longer sold for national distribution, international sales agents today make a big part of their money by asking for screening fees from festivals. So the Galaxy also represents an aggregate of potential clients. Therefore, festival screening fees have increased at an impressive rate in the past five years – from €200 to €2,000 in some cases. At the same time, the sales agents are the greatest powers in today's Galaxy, the ones who possess the ability to determine the circulation of films. With the passage of time, this power has passed from government bureaucrats to producers and distributors, and, finally, to the agents. Now the Galaxy is more chaotic than in its previous phases; but its power is no less firm.

And, what's more, the Galaxy has a centre: the Cannes Film Festival. The modern era of film festivals and of programming as a more or less transparent activity began when Cannes made the decision to become sovereign in its programming – that it was going to invite the films that its programming committee selected – thus ending the era when films were submitted by nation-states or by film industry organisations. But, since that time, Cannes has also increasingly become the place where the fate of all independent and non-Hollywood cinema is decided. Not the fate of Indian cinema, certainly, with its one thousand productions per year that seldom make it to the West, but of all cinema that aspires to be seen anywhere besides its country of origin. In addition, the evolution of film festivals marks a change in the idea of cosmopolitanism that had always been associated with international showcases of culture. The most important change during those years is that festivals evolved from exhibiting the films that each country wished to show and began instead, and as if creating a new international language, promoting a notion of 'international cinema' based on works shown in festivals.

Getting back to Cannes: every year that festival exhibits as 'world premieres' approximately a hundred films (adding up the titles in all sections). These world premieres generate critical reaction that will influence the films' prestige and acceptability and, in a very definitive manner, their movement through the Galaxy. The status of each individual film depends strongly on the assessment of the critics and on the fomentation of the distributors present in Cannes. The audience certainly does not influence the fate of films, since at Cannes there are hardly any audiences beyond the Côte d'Azur bourgeoisie invited to the gala events. But the careers of a good many directors from around the world depend on what happens to them at Cannes. There, some filmmakers achieve access to big-time production possibilities, to US money. Others simply guarantee their survival. Once, while I was in Cannes, I had the task of interviewing Jean-Luc Godard who was presenting a film in competition. A bit surprised, I asked him what he was doing there. He responded that his producer had requested that he attend the festival in order to acquire funding for his next film. As is well known, Cannes is also a market and, above all, a marketplace into the future. But for people such as Manoel de Oliveira, Apichatpong Weerasethakul, Lisandro Alonso, Béla Tarr or Albert Serra, survival in the motion-picture industry depends (or did very strongly at a given moment in their careers) on Cannes, on the reception of their films there, and on the contacts and agreements that they were able to achieve by attending that festival. Vancouver and Vienna, Hong Kong and São Paulo, Lisbon and Yerevan will structure the programming of their own festival around a nucleus of films screened at Cannes. Cannes is a sun whose rays reach all sectors of the Galaxy, while Venice (especially), Berlin, Toronto and Rotterdam are lesser stars that likewise possess their own orbiting planets. Hundreds of programmers visit these festivals to select what they will show in their own festivals. It's almost impossible for a medium-sized festival to have the means to discover a film, unless that discovery takes place in another festival. In order for a motion picture to be seen internationally, the only possibilities are to find an American studio that will take on distribution via its worldwide affiliates, or to enter into circulation in the Galaxy by way of a festival that is more or less important.

Although infinitely interconnected, the Galaxy is not a cooperative network. Overpopulation creates a struggle for space and paranoia vis-à-vis neighbours. The struggle among festivals to be the first to present films, or to present them exclusively, is one of the wars in the Galaxy. Festivals are dying to get a premiere – a world, international, continental, national, provincial, municipal premiere – deploying seduction, bribery, pressure, and blackmail in order to succeed in their endeavours. It would seem that premieres attract international press attention, even though it is not at all clear exactly why this presence is important to a festival that is only oriented towards a local audience – as the majority of festivals are. The rivalry with other film festivals becomes the most important concern for those in charge. Venice's artistic director dreams about her/his peer at Cannes. But in Rome, they're dreaming about Venice. And Locarno. And San Sebastián. And in Rotterdam, they're dreaming about Locarno. And in Amsterdam (a documentary film festival), about Marseille (another documentary film festival). And in Marseille, about Cinéma du Réel in Paris (a third documentary film festival). And in Guadalajara, about FICCO in Mexico City. And in Mar del Plata, about BAFICI. And in Montreal the World Film Festival worries about Toronto – or the other festival in Montreal, the Festival Nouveau Cinéma. And in Valladolid, they dream about San Sebastián; and in San Sebastián, about Gijón, which is on the way up and is younger and more modern…

2. Being There

I don't have a clear explanation for this widespread situation, which ends up being a nightmare. I participated in that nightmare during the four years that I was the director of BAFICI, from 2000 to 2004. In the beginning, it was easy: the national government, in charge of Mar del Plata believed that what a festival needed was pomp, government support, Category A status and, in passing, all sorts of deals with producers, embassies and liaison agents for stars, former stars or pseudo stars. Mar del Plata's management paid Catherine Deneuve $50,000 to attend for two days and, by manipulating access to state support for production, put pressure on Argentine filmmakers to present their films at that venue. It was the typical festival from another era – official, antiquated, bureaucratic and tied to the red-carpet traditions and the trotting out of dubious stars on opening night. It was the notion of a film festival as dreamt up by cultural bureaucrats in Argentina and in so many other countries. At times, strictly by chance, some good films got shown. The festival that I was tapped to direct, BAFICI, was born under a good star in 1999. It was conceived by the municipal authorities to challenge Mar del Plata on the basis of a certain modernity, and bearing in mind the environment of a capital city, including certain cultural traditions which held sway amongst the citizenry, particularly the cinephiles. There had never been a festival in Buenos Aires, an enormous city with a signifi- cant middle class. BAFICI could not help but grow at a rapid pace. When I was appointed to direct it (after the previous director had been fired because of political pettiness, just as I would be eventually), the festival had already been launched; and it was on the verge of an explosion that was clearly inevitable. The day I began to work with a group of four programmers – a mere four months before the 2001 edition of the festival – I had no idea about such elementary things as the economic and physical trajectories that motion pictures follow before finally arriving on screen.

Nevertheless, it was a very easy task. We were able to choose 200 feature films with no restrictions or compromises whatsoever. Outside our doors was an audience waiting for us to show them something that they had not seen before. Pretty much anything they hadn't seen before. Very few people in that audience had heard of Béla Tarr, Hou Hsiao-Hsien or Pedro Costa, or of new Korean directors like Hong Sang-soo, Lee Chang-dong or Bong Joon-ho. On the other hand, I knew perfectly well that Jia Zhangke's *Plat- form* had to win the international competition (reserved for first and second works) in the festival's up-coming edition. I knew this even though I had not yet seen *Platform*. In the first edition of BAFICI, in 1999, his outstanding first work, *Xiao-wu*, had been screened in a 16mm print but went unnoticed. The second film by that extraordinary director had to become emblematic of our first programme. It wasn't a question of manipulating the jury towards that end; all that was necessary was to choose the jury members in an appropriate manner. So my first decision was to invite Jonathan Rosenbaum to be a jury member. *Platform* couldn't lose. What I didn't know was that it was not so easy to succeed in finally getting the film exhibited, because it had changed sales agents since its presentation at Venice. During the course of three months of faxes (we still used those in the office), e-mails and phone calls, I discovered what the really hard work of a festival was: negotiating with the holders of the rights, especially when one has limited means.

In truth, I was always convinced that the critics were our secret weapons. During the three months we had to prepare the festival, we were only able to go to Rotterdam and see a limited number of films. However, a network of friends gave us sufficient information and recommendations to be able to mount the programme. Fortunately, in previous years, without ever thinking that we would some day be in charge of a festival, we had cultivated the friendship of a group of critics and programmers – among them Simon Field, then director of Rotterdam and another member of our first jury. Being individuals who were the most tuned-in, this group became the spoiled guests of our following editions. Those who had been jury members wrote for the catalogue and curated retrospectives for us gratis. The BAFICI catalogues from those years were written by some of the best pens in the cinema business – I remember, among many others and in addition to Rosenbaum, Adrian Martin, Mark Peranson, Nicole Brenez, Jim Hoberman, Kent Jones, Olaf Möller. We even published several books under their names. Suddenly, almost without having tried, and thanks to the festival's guests, we had succeeded in creating an ambience that was passionately cinephile. That first year was magic. Jim Jarmusch, a legendary figure in independent cinema worthy of Mme Tussaud's, attended. Olivier Assayas and Maggie Cheung, who were an item at the time, came. I even had the pleasure of sending an e-mail to Assayas telling him that I would be pleased if he came, but even more so if Maggie (my favourite actress) could come. The Minister of Culture (and future mayor of Buenos Aires) put a chauffeured automobile at the disposition of Jarmusch; however, this nicety was not budgeted for in the case of Maggie and Olivier, since the Minister had never heard of them. So my brother-in-law was charged with driving them around in our ancient Volkswagen. During those four editions of BAFICI my wife Flavia worked elbow to elbow with me – that was one of the greatest pleasures of those absurd years.

The little star in the south of the American continent had suddenly grown in size in the Galaxy, and I had the sensation of having organised a party. Audiences were enchanted and, against all the conservatism of the press and against the industry pundits, they were ready to watch what we put in front of them. The works of Johnny To and Takashi Miike, two filmmakers who were absolutely unknown to me, created a sensation. We discovered that an underground network of fanatics exchanged videos of their films. Bruce La Bruce had become an idol of the gay community in Buenos Aires and we had to schedule screenings of his films at three in the morning. There are many fond memories. I recall, for example, Naomi Kawase dressed in traditional Japanese attire the day her film won a prize. *The Mad Songs of Fernanda Hussein*, John Gianvito's first film, had its international premiere in Buenos Aires and also won a prize. That last day I realised that we had achieved an extraordinary success.

La libertad by Lisandro Alonso had its world premiere in the third edition of BAFICI. A few months before, a timid and gawky youth had given me a cassette saying, 'I'd like you to take a look at this stuff that I filmed.' When I did so, I fell over backwards. It was the best film that I'd seen from the recent Argentine cinema, which was then undergoing a very interesting period. Immediately I thought that this film was going to be one of the highlights of the competition, a film that would justify any international critic or programmer making the trip to Buenos Aires. But several days later, Christian Jeune, a representative of the Cannes Film Festival, saw the film and selected it for Cannes' *Un Certain Regard* showcase. This choice astonished the head of INCAA (the official film institution in Argentina) and also local producers, who contended that *La libertad* exemplified the sort of elite cinema whose production should be discouraged in Argentina. In fact, the project had not received any sort of official support. Once the film was selected for Cannes, the rules prohibited it from being shown in other festivals, even in Argentina. It was only after lengthy negotiations that I succeeded in getting permission for a single screening during BAFICI – and this only on the condition that it be shown out of competition. That's when I understood that Cannes was so powerful that it could even block the screening of films in their own countries of origin. The Galaxy was flexing its hierarchical muscle.

In 2002, Argentina crashed. The economy had been rapidly declining, and it underwent a shock. Argentine currency lost two-thirds of its value; bank accounts were frozen; unemployment soared to 25 per cent; people protested in the streets, and they were bartering goods in makeshift markets. The Festival's budget was reduced to some $150,000, a fifth of the previous year's. Nevertheless, our popularity in the Galaxy remained high: we had managed to please everybody. Particularly Jacques Gerber (at that time programmer for Cannes' Directors' Fortnight) – he organised a campaign of economic support for us. Various festivals transferred funds to us; sales agents did not charge us their screening fees; many people personally paid their travel costs in order to attend; and, even though the ATM machines of Buenos Aires were not paying out any bills and businesses were not accepting credit cards, the festival came off perfectly. Spectators flocked to see films by Straub & Huillet and Pedro Costa, while the world outside was going up in flames. It was as if cinema had become a site of resistance to adversity, a place of hope – as if cinema had recovered a status lost long ago. Those days were some of the strangest of my life.

Afterwards, everything became a little duller. Slowly, the country began to get its economy back on track; and, once the Festival had assured its position in the Galaxy, its novelty wore off. What, precisely, was this status that we had achieved? A wide range of answers was possible. For our part, we had carved out a vanguard position in the Galaxy: we were showing the edgiest cinema that could be seen at that time, we had contracted no obligations, and our relationship with the audience was splendid. Instead of waiting for the same old things, every year people would ask us what new and strange things we were going to dream up for them; and the press stopped asking which celebrities would be invited. We differed from other festivals in that we attempted to have the outer reaches of international cinema occupy our festival's centre stage on an equal footing. We banished categories such as 'documentary section', 'midnight movies', and 'experimental cinema' – mere ghettos for a certain sector of the audience. Nor, of course, did we allow 'galas', 'masterpieces', or anything of the kind that might imply the recognition of a pre-established hierarchy for the films that we were showing. The challenge was to outdo ourselves, and we were, I have to admit, inching a bit in the direction of the snobbishness that had changed BAFICI into a place to be – something that happens in many other parts of the Galaxy. Film festivals are almost always 'cool'. This is not a cynical expression: after all, the audience that fills up the theatres does not consist exclusively of cognoscenti nor of hardcore cinephiles. But, in turn, it's no good making concessions in order to fill up theatres. In the offerings of film festivals there are no true blockbusters, unless one programmes the very movies that are going to open in commercial cinemas the following week.

3. *Goodfellas*

Not long ago, someone told me that the most pleasing thing about BAFICI was that, when going to breakfast in a festival hotel, one did not meet disagreeable people. Some days later, a member of a panel in Austria defined the work of a festival director as a series of actions aimed at strengthening what she labeled 'a nice mafia'. Both perspectives contain elements of truth. Because the true war in the Galaxy – far more significant than the disputes amongst festivals – is the battle amongst tribes that resembles a metaphysical struggle between good and evil. It's not that good is only found on one side, but rather that evil is found on many sides. In the final instance, what distinguishes one guest from another at the breakfast table is the same thing that separates a noble film from a film that pretends to be noble and thus, by pretending nobility, participates in the circuit of films more or less detached from the mainstream of festival films. It's the difference that exists between *Taste of Cherry* by Abbas Kiarostami and *Irreversible* by Gaspar Noé. It's clear that, even though they live together day to day in the Galaxy, essentially, admirers of one film share very little in common with those who admire the other. Both films competed at Cannes, and that's where the problems start.

I clearly remember various conversations I had with Thierry Frémaux, the *délégué artistique* from Cannes. His conception of the official programme required the representation of all types of film production and, therefore, the type of films made by Kiarostami, Hong Sang-soo, Pedro Costa, Apichatpong Weerasethakul, Jia Zhangke, or even Oliveira. However, this type of film can only have limited space in the competition – at most two or three slots – while all the other slots have to be for movies that are more conventional, narratively orthodox, and that present 'important' subjects or perhaps even mildly scandalous themes (that's where *Irreversible* would come in). The aforementioned films by Kiarostami *et al.* can even win the Palme d'Or; but they never receive a gala screening since they are usually shown just once, at four o'clock in the afternoon to a half-empty house.

Frémaux's argument is that the most difficult films, the most rigorous ones, need the *cannoise* paraphernalia in order to exist. Frémaux argues, in short, that the flashiest and most commercial movies end up protecting works that are more fragile, because the latter benefit from the attention of the press and from the framework of glamour that the festival offers. It's possible that he may have a point there. Nevertheless, given that Cannes has succeeded in imposing on the world an idea of cinema that certainly encompasses very diverse and even opposing aesthetic tendencies, it would be interesting to know if a radicalisation of the Cannes selection process might improve the quality of what the Galaxy has to offer. Or, must we heed the voices clamouring from all quarters that Cannes continue to bow before the populist altar of a supposed market, one that 'shows the public what it wants'? In fact, it's unusual for a film in Cannes, even a winner, to make money unless a studio takes an interest in distributing it. As we have already indicated, in Cannes there is no audience; but the majority of those who attend the gala events in the Lumière Theatre believe in that sort of mythology.

In other words, if a change in the demographic makeup were to leave the tribe of those who believe in Gaspar Noé outside of the Galaxy and only include the tribe of Kiarostami aficionados, the Galaxy would become a much less populated but more agreeable place, something like the breakfast room that we had successfully created in BAFICI. It seems as if that would be really easy, if Cannes would only take the initiative. But that is unlikely to happen. It was even difficult in Buenos Aires. Let me explain. On the one hand, it is not very easy to distinguish between a cinephile and a 'body snatcher' of a cinephile, i.e. one of those persons who appears agreeable and knowledgeable, but who turns out to regard cinema with the mentality of a Harvey Weinstein. And, on the other hand, there are the funding problems. When I assumed the directorship of BAFICI, we had the idea of inviting producers, distributors and managers of economic development funds to Buenos Aires and of organising co-production meetings that included workshops, seminars, and so on. All this in order to assist the New Argentine Cinema. That's how a parade of supposedly well-intentioned individuals came to Buenos Aires, all quite concerned that Latin American filmmakers be able to gain access to international financing. This is, in fact, what happened; and today there are many Argentine directors who, in addition to government assistance from their own country, are benefitting from co-production arrangements with France, Germany, Switzerland and particularly Spain. This has not improved the quality of the films, but has enormously increased their cost. The films of the young Argentine directors are no longer fresh and original, as they were ten years ago; and their films have now become part and parcel of the rather colourless mediocrity produced by economic development funds and co-production money.

An additional consequence of this process is that the Argentine filmmakers, who in other times used to attend festivals in order to enjoy the trip and find out what was being done elsewhere, are today preoccupied with obtaining money. The spiritual deterioration of the Rotterdam festival is notable in this regard ever since Cinemart, its co-production market, took over the event, and the place filled up in a few years with sales agents, distributors and representatives of television networks on one side, and, on the other, with mendicant filmmakers attempting to sell their projects. This all adds up to an infernal machine dedicated to constantly churning out counterfeits of interesting, free-spirited, edgy and rigorous films. These days I believe a festival is better if it doesn't have markets of any kind and producers don't assist.

The Galaxy harbours one of its principal enemies within its own reproductive apparatus. Festivals are plagued with people who represent a 'bad mafia' that conspires to produce conventional and mediocre cinema while concealing that same cinema's impoverishment, thanks to the consensus of those who manufacture similar products and thanks to critics schooled in complacency. Unlike the old movie houses, which were completely separate from the places where pictures were financed, film festivals are also the itinerant base of the new cinema merchants with their mechanisms that control and dominate the production and reproduction of an adulterated art. If there is one thing I regret during those years with BAFICI, it's having allowed access to a part of the 'bad mafia' – the part dedicated to this kind of new colonisation of the Third World. It's too late for regrets. At any rate, San Clemente continues on without a festival; and for three years now, I have been out of the Galaxy. Maybe things have changed a lot since I left.

The Sandwich Process: Simon Field Talks About Polemics and Poetry at Film Festivals

JAMES QUANDT

'I'm rather grey' was Simon Field's typically droll response when asked how I would recognise him at the 1993 Toronto Film Festival, since we knew each other only via missive. Then film curator and distributor for the Institute of Contemporary Arts in London, Simon was a daunting colleague whose taste and expertise extended from the most recondite experimental cinema to the wild-ass baroquery of Japanese B-director Seijun Suzuki. When Simon ascended to the role of director of the Rotterdam Film Festival in 1996, the 'happy few' atmosphere of that event – a sort of seaport cinephile salon with small films and blessedly few industry types – changed dramatically. In the eight years he remained in the position before decamping in a fog of regret and rumour – was he pushed, many wondered, by parochial powers who wanted a more home-team, Dutch-speaking director? – the Rotterdam festival turned from an intimate mid-winter gathering whose compact programme reflected the tastes of one man, and where directors, critics, curators and the film-going public rubbed shoulders at communal dinners in the tiny Central Hotel, to a vast event where, as at Rotterdam's hitherto anti-models (Toronto, Berlin), many curators got to exert their penchants, and hits from

Hubert Bals, founder of the International Film Festival Rotterdam.

the festival circuit played in multiplex cinemas to throngs of eager audiences. It became, to use one of Simon's favourite phrases, a more plural festival, incorporating everyone from Ernie Gehr to Claude Chabrol. The latter's *Rien ne va plus* furnished a scrap of scandal when Simon gave it pride of place at the 1997 festival, the local stalwarts outraged not because it was a weak film, which it was, but because Chabrol simply did not qualify as Rotterdam material, his renown contradictory to the modest, exploratory tenor of the festival established by its legendary founder, Hubert Bals, in whose long shadow all successive directors laboured. Simon was a purist but also a pluralist, and the festival benefited from his capacious taste. (Dinners, however, maintained that old Rotterdam vibe, even in more exclusive settings. At one repast for Takeshi Kitano, a young assistant succumbed to either jet lag or the city's tokable pleasures, passing out face first in his plate, black mane set ablaze by a candle. As the reek of singed hair mingled with rijstaffel and we leapt to douse the flames, Kitano looked on impassively, bored or bemused it was hard to tell.) The heartfelt plaudits and tears that accompanied Simon's farewell at Rotterdam were a measure of the respect and fondness which he stirred in filmmakers, critics and cinephiles.

When we recently met for this interview on an unseasonably cold mid-September Saturday in 2007 over stale sashimi and gumboot grilled squid, I hoped that our vexed positions – Simon as (then) director of international programming for the Dubai Film Festival, I as an employee of the Toronto festival – would not stanch honest discussion. No doubt because he has played so many roles in the film world – curator, critic, distributor, festival director and, most recently, producer (of the prodigious *New Crowned Hope* cycle) – Simon revealed an expansive insight into the functions of festivals, and an ability to see issues from various viewpoints. I counted more than a dozen instances in which he used the phrase 'on the other hand', most edited out in the following text, but a sure indicator of Simon's complex perspective. Though he prizes polemics and is known for his impeccable principles, he expressed surprising leniency over some issues that critics of film festivals have battened onto, paired with an acerbic understanding of how power too often obviates poetry at events supposedly dedicated to an art.

James Quandt: You have just come off back-to-back festivals, Venice, reportedly the oldest in the world, and Toronto. How do the festivals, the respective experiences, compare, and how have they changed over the time you have been attending each?

Simon Field: I have been attending Toronto for something like twenty years, since I was a programmer at the ICA. I haven't been attending Venice as long, only since the time I went to Rotterdam as director. In terms of changes, I'm much more aware of the Toronto changes. Venice clearly shifts under different directors, for instance the feeling how under Marco Müller there is a cinephile element that was not so strong before, but that's obviously debatable. He was preceded by the very estimable Alberto Barbera. There haven't been enormous changes in scale there, perhaps more emphasis on Hollywood, getting caught up in the cycle of those international release schedules. But that of course brings us straight back to Toronto, which has clearly got substantially larger since I first came. To my mind, the whole conception of the galas and special presentations has begun to dominate the festival, they have become more of a priority and Toronto, whether it likes it or not, has got caught up in the marketing procedures, particularly of Hollywood but also of the independent American cinema machine. Some of the auteurist emphases of the older festival have begun to get a little lost, though if you look at the 2007 edition it has Lav Diaz, it has Manoel de Oliveira. The masters *are* there. In the time I have been coming, it has become a much bigger machine, emphasising more and more its premieres. It's become much more self-conscious about being one of the most important festivals in the world; it's more preoccupied with its own rhetoric, celebrating its rhetoric. On the other hand, they have had for some years the 'Wavelengths' programme and now have this 'Future Projections' programme, so that while it has become a showcase for Hollywood and its release patterns, there's an attempt to pay more attention to the avant-garde. But I'm not sure what's happened to the films in the middle ground, what lies between.

JQ: An acquaintance, who's been attending the Toronto festival for twenty-five years, recently told me this was the year she decided she was giving up because it has become so caught up in star-fucking that she was fed up with it. I responded that she can just ignore the glitz, it has nothing to do with her, and she can find her own festival. She's particularly interested in documentaries, and there's a strong slate here. The cliché is that with festivals this size, anybody can find what they're looking for. Why even be concerned about Hollywood and the galas at a festival this size, or at Cannes for that matter?

SF: In the Netherlands, there's what they call the 'sandwich process', how you use bigger films to get audiences to support your festival and its smaller – but equally important – films. They become not an alibi so much as a support system. You need the profile in the press, which comes with the big films and the films that are being sold to local distributors. They become a rationale that drives the festival, at all sorts of levels: they are the films the audiences often want to see, they represent the interests of the studios and the independents; they are, sadly, what the press wants to cover. The danger is that the balance begins to shift. How do you keep that balance? In the case of Rotterdam, we were not troubled by stars because we were not on the circuit, we were not part of the machinery. In Toronto, it has begun to affect the tone of the festival and one of its roles, a role of which much is made here, to educate and inform, and the problem is how to maintain that balance when, for instance, all films are described as fabulous, and when some parts of the festival disappear beneath an overcrowded programme. The noise of the 'upper' part of the festival drowns out other areas. When you get the feeling that rhetoric, and the marketers have taken over, you begin to be concerned that the marginal films aren't at the centre of anyone's interest.

JQ: I think the festival would argue, because they have been very concerned about this trend and this criticism, that they have attempted to address it by, for instance, starting the festival daily, their own publication, and making sure that at least ninety per cent of it is directed towards the films that don't otherwise get much coverage, the smaller films. They have made a concerted effort to compensate for the media's attention on stars and Hollywood.

SF: Which is absolutely correct. We tried to do the same thing with the Daily in Rotterdam because a similar problem occurs there. Veteran visionary directors of the independent cinema like Werner Schroeter and Tonino De Bernardi are now marginal directors even at a festival like Rotterdam. You have to ensure they get that coverage, but as a festival gets bigger it becomes harder and harder to create that attention – which filmmakers does one choose to feature in the Daily among so many deserving cases?

JQ: To go back to Lav Diaz, what do you do as a festival director with a nine-hour Filipino film? At the screening yesterday, there were about ten people in a 34-seat cinema. A question that always arises is how to present a film like that so it has an audience, so that people don't feel that they are giving up three or four other films to see it.

SF: I don't think there is an answer to the last part of your question. All of us become intoxicated with the attempt to see as many films as possible, but that's also one of the consequences of a festival becoming gargantuan. After I left Rotterdam, I had the fantasy of doing a festival of perhaps 25 films. What people always talked about nostalgically at Rotterdam was the time when the audience would have seen most of the films at the festival together, you know, 'I remember sitting on the steps of the Lanteren cinema with Fassbinder.' It's tinged by a certain sentimentality, but the point is valid. We need more of the Telluride types of festivals, where there is a tough gatekeeper. If you present a Lav Diaz in a festival like that, it's very different from one where there are 350 films. It does affect the likelihood of people wanting to see the film. I always defended the size of Rotterdam, using the same grounds you described earlier, that people can find their own way through the festival. Some people go to see films from developing countries or experimental cinema, and then some of the audience sees maybe ten films which are essentially previews since they'll go into distribution before long. I always defended making that kind of mixture – following that 'sandwich' formula – a polyphonic festival. But when I left and went back as a member of the public, I realised how that size was disadvantageous. You run into problems even if you have a daily to support filmmakers, like De Bernardi, but whose audience is fifteen, twenty people.

JQ: You raise something interesting, which is the difference between your perception of a festival as a director and the same event as a member of the public. When you were director at Rotterdam, did you try to see it from the other perspective?

SF: Yes, we were all concerned about that, but it's very hard to cut down a festival, for several reasons. You have a very large public who want to see the films. You have a certain number of theatres you want to fill. In the case of Rotterdam, you also have programmers, all claiming they have several fabulous films they must include. We did discuss the matter of size at Rotterdam and when I left, Sandra den Hamer[1] did try to cut it down substantially. They did reduce the number of films, but the festival didn't seem any smaller. If you take the catholic approach, you're showing the diversity of cinema for different motivations and different audiences, but at the time it's very hard to contain. This explains not just the growing size of festivals, but the growing number of them.

JQ: There's an old *New Yorker* cartoon of two men surveying a rocky crag in the middle of nowhere and one of them saying, 'What this place needs is a film festival', and it seems like that has become true, and I don't mean Telluride. *Variety* reports that the number of festivals in the world is reaching 500, though that number seems small – there must be 500 annual festivals in Toronto alone. What explains this proliferation?

SF: Cities or countries want to have film festivals, cultural organisations see it as a focus for sponsorship, or for bringing glamorous people: there are reasons that people who are not film-involved want a festival. Producers and filmmakers obviously desire a showcase for their films. There is also the cinephile motivation. Do I think it's a good thing? It's a circular discussion. For instance, if you're in Des Moines and the chances of seeing a wide range of international cinema are very low, who are we to refuse that public the chance to see films from Thailand or Russia? Even if it's a mainstream festival, many of those films don't get distributed, so it seems rather cruel to suggest that those festivals shouldn't exist. On the other hand, there is a bad side to this proliferation. When we talk about Toronto, Rotterdam, Cannes, they're all competing with each other and we know now that Toronto is very much preoccupied with world premieres. Rumour has it that it prevents other festivals from getting films, which is characteristic of every festival that wants to have premieres, to stop others from getting them first. This cannot be good for filmmakers, or help their films getting seen widely. If you're an Iranian filmmaker, for example, and you put all your eggs in the Berlin basket, which means your film can't be shown in Rotterdam, in whose interest is that? The festival can say, of course, that it *is* in the interest of the filmmaker because if it's a world premiere, the press come to see it. It's quite clear that for a certain kind of cinema now distribution is through festivals and not through theatres.

JQ: Does the proliferation of festivals serve film culture?

SF: The answer has to be both yes and no. We've moved more and more into an event culture. Despite whatever is said about DVD, people do want to be part of a gathering, and they look to a gatekeeper such as a festival curator to determine that experience. And as a festival gets bigger, that gatekeeper role gets lost.

JQ: By gatekeeper, you mean people are looking for a curator's 'seal of approval'?

SF: Yes. It's one of the interesting debates about the proliferation of DVD: how do people know what they should look at when they're very busy and have so many demands on their time?

JQ: Cinematheque programmers joke that as our vocation becomes quickly extinct, our future will be as house-to-house consultants on programming home theatres.

SF: 'It's Mr. Quandt at the door, mom!'

JQ: 'Tell him to go away! We don't want any more Pedro Costa!'

SF: But the event thing is very important, in gaining momentum to get, for example, press coverage. Critics will write about a film in a festival they would otherwise ignore during the year.

JQ: How many festivals in the world pay screening fees? They don't like to talk about it, it's kind of a dirty secret, and how does that affect the system of distribution and exhibition? There's a sense that film festivals are rapidly replacing year-round exhibition.

SF: The latter is certainly the case. Having had the experience of producing *New Crowned Hope*, we were working with some of the most important filmmakers in the world, but for their work to get sold theatrically has become increasingly difficult. I don't think that's a consequence of the growth of festivals. Other factors are cutting into arthouse distribution and cinema circuits. There is an alternative circuit of festivals growing up, and the majority of those 500 festivals are now having to pay rentals. The bigger sales agents will let films go free to a festival they regard as creating a showcase or a sales potential, and I would imagine that Sundance, Toronto, Cannes, Rotterdam generally don't pay rentals. Many of the rest do. For instance, I know that *I Don't Want to Sleep Alone* and *Syndromes and a Century* got maybe fifty or sixty festival bookings. *Grabvica*, a film which won the Golden Bear in Berlin, had something like a hundred bookings in one year. You need staff to tend to the bookings and prints, so they're quite justified in charging rentals. It's also becoming another source of income for films that aren't selling as broadly as they once did.

JQ: It used to be the case that European festivals were largely supported by the state, but increasingly that funding is going and they're having to scramble to make it up, and some festivals are doing better than others at it. To use that globalising term, 'it's a new world', and it has been difficult, at Berlin in particular. In an open letter to you about your departure from Rotterdam, the Dutch critic Hans Beerekamp wrote, 'The festival risks becoming a management-driven event, with enough bums on seats, happy sponsors and happy distributors.' Having gone to Rotterdam for years, I laughed and wondered what he would make of North American festivals! Do you think sponsorship has an effect on film festivals, the way it does in museums and symphony orchestras? Did it affect Rotterdam in any way?

SF: Rotterdam was and is very lucky in having strong institutional and government backing. One-third of the budget was grant aid, one-third was public, and the rest was one-off grants and sponsorship. It was getting harder and harder to get sponsorship even while I was at the festival. Sponsorship did not shape the programme in Rotterdam. The sponsorship department always wanted one or two films they could show to sponsors, but they were films that were already part of that 'sandwich' I've talked about.

JQ: What about the stories we hear about major festivals in which films are selected because they are 'bundled' by producers or sales agents or companies with desirable films? In other words: 'Yes, you can have that film for competition, but you also have to take this one', and it's not a film the festival wants, or is even embarrassed to show. There was a famous instance at Rotterdam where a major Dutch distributor who handled a whole slate of films you had selected for the festival made the deal contingent on showing one film you didn't want, and you had to negotiate. Is it inevitable that every festival faces a situation like that?

SF: It doesn't happen very often. In Rotterdam, as I'm sure happens at other festivals, if you have a sales agent or distributor who wants to showcase his films, then they can put pressure on you, but there's always going to be degrees of negotiation, particularly if a distributor has a number of films you want. But I would be very surprised if a certain amount of trading-off didn't happen between festivals like Cannes and Toronto and powerful sales agents or studios. I sometimes wonder what happens with, for instance, a company like Mongrel Media that has a very substantial slate of films here in Toronto.

JQ: Since you bring it up, Mongrel kept *Taste of Cherry* the year it won the Palme d'Or at Cannes out of the Toronto festival, arguing that its audience would be used up at the festival, that even in a city like Toronto the audience for a film like that is limited and that everyone who wanted to see it would do so at the festival and nothing would remain when it opened commercially. They stuck to that decision despite remonstration, and the festival lost a very important film.

SF: That is a very common discussion. It probably doesn't come up with Cannes, but certainly with Rotterdam it did, and having been a distributor, I have some sympathy with their view. If you show a film in Rotterdam's Pathé cinema and then in two smaller cinemas, there is the possibility of a thousand people seeing it. With a lot of these arthouse titles, the potential audience is maybe five or six thousand, and you can really understand when someone says that is going to eat into their profits. Festivals argue that they're showing all the important films of the year and feel bereft if one is denied them. I know some festivals have always paid some percentage of the box office to the distributors or the sales agents and that may happen more and more, and that somewhat compensates. A distributor who puts a film into this festival or Cannes or Rotterdam doesn't see any money from it. The question is what do they get from it? You know the Toronto market better than I do, but I expect the situation is quite common.

JQ: There certainly are films that I do not consider as a limited run at the Cinematheque after the festival for those very reasons. Believe it or not, it's an important factor for us at the Cinematheque for a limited run to be a Toronto premiere, because it hasn't lost its audience to the festival.

SF: You're exactly in the position I've been talking about.

JQ: Festivals are becoming more numerous, but they're also becoming omnivorous – they seem to want to do everything. Cannes has added a large classics or restoration sidebar, for instance, which presents a real conflict for someone like me who would rather be there, but is in Cannes to see new films. The Bologna festival already exists for exhibiting restorations. Other festivals, perhaps taking their cue from Rotterdam and its 'Exploding Cinema' programme, which was very important for you when you were director of that festival, have added either sidebars of avant-garde or experimental cinema, as the New York Film Festival has done for some years and Toronto more recently with 'Wavelengths'. Toronto also added a sidebar of film/video installations this year. Why does cinema need to be 'exploded', and do you think more festivals should go in this direction?

SF: 'Exploding Cinema' existed before I got to Rotterdam, largely because of Kees Kasander.[2] It was partly to do with technological developments and being open to new 'genres' of work, by which I mean the video promo, which was beginning to be taken seriously, but also the beginnings of digital media and the presentation of films in art galleries. I expanded on that, partly because I had my own interest in the visual arts, partly because of my experience at the ICA and the discussions there about how digital art was changing delivery systems and artistic conceptions. So I think in the case of Rotterdam it was absolutely essential for a festival whose essence was innovation and new directions in cinema to be open to those new directions. There is, as you suggest, a question about the coherence of the programming. I think some programmers in this area think it's automatically interesting if the work is digital or new media. 'Evidently, something is happening, Mr. Jones, and you don't know what it is.' You get it with all kinds of crossovers with advertising or music that can be unprincipled. On the other hand, I do think some of the filmmakers we have worked with over the years, Michael Snow is an example, because they have their feet in both worlds, have explored how to present cinema in different formats. There are many Snow pieces that are made for the gallery but can be absolutely considered 'cinema'. And other filmmakers, Guy Maddin comes to mind,[3] who have jumped over the fence between cinema and art, for reasons that might have to do with prestige, or exploring different ways of presenting work or formats, and a festival like Rotterdam has to respond to that. That's why we broached the question of 'What is Cinema?'

JQ: Historically, film festivals have played a role in establishing and, conversely, stalling or damaging directors' reputations and careers. Certain

Japanese studios were attentive to Western festivals (Venice especially) so Ozu, Mizoguchi, Kurosawa became known, but other Japanese directors were not shown, so remained obscure outside of home. But I am more concerned about, for example, how Theo Angelopoulos was not shown at NYFF or TIFF. Richard Roud was reportedly against him, and I think that established a tradition. So the Angelopoulos retro at the Museum of Modern Art in the 1990s was the first intensive look at his work there, and did much to establish him in the pantheon. Whatever one thinks of him, he's important. Ditto Werner Schroeter. Toronto promoted Lothar Lambert (who he?) with a retro, but did not show Schroeter. The New York Film Festival also ignored him. He is still largely unknown in North America as a consequence, though he's one of the greatest directors ever. On the other hand, Toronto promoted Bob Swaim and Pierre Jolivet as the next big French auteurs, but who cares about them now? At the same time, Philippe Garrel was never shown, except at the Montreal festival, so he also remains in obscurity here. The examples could go on. I don't know if Rotterdam has consistently ignored anyone important, but it does have a perverse allegiance to certain filmmakers, such as Tonino De Bernardi. Then Cannes seems to feel obliged to put every new Kusturica in competition, each more intolerable than the last…

SF: I doubt whether we can make anything significant out of the second part of your argument, about preventing great filmmakers from being celebrated or the audience they deserve, because in a way, there are always figures in the history of cinema who won't get the attention we think they deserve. Festivals can be blamed to an extent, but it's part of a whole process, which films are written about. Critics can also ignore important films.

JQ: But isn't that where critics see films, at festivals? So that becomes a circular, self-perpetuating process.

SF: Yeah, it does. But the negative examples are more difficult to talk about. Festivals can be negative to a whole type of cinema. Most festivals are negative to the directors we consider the best in the world. To me it's the other side of the argument: can they over-promote people? Or keep people in circulation who should not be?

JQ: Names?

SF: (Laughs) I'm sure you can provide your own list, much more caustic than mine. There's also the matter of the principles of curating a festival. At Rotterdam, the 'Filmmakers in Focus' programme[4] was very important in drawing attention to directors who were underestimated, not just by the public but also by the critics, because two out of three of the directors would elicit questions from the Dutch critics: 'Who on earth is this person?' The attitude being if I haven't heard of him or her it must be a bad choice. But I think that makes it a good choice.

JQ: Which again points out the importance of film festivals in establishing, or not, a director's reputation because many of the retrospectives you organised went on to be shown at many other venues, including our cinematheque. Anne-Marie Miéville, Fukasaku, I can name any number of the ones you did which introduced several of us curators or programmers to their work. I agree that cinematheques also play that role, and can also revive a reputation, but they play a smaller role than festivals.

SF: Not smaller necessarily. I think there is an analogy between what is done at cinematheques and what can be done at festivals. Festivals should have a *parti pris*, they should have a type of cinema they want to support and to propose, of course that's a very Rotterdam 'position'. It's not the London Film Festival position. Toronto had it much more early on when it did director or national spotlights. It has now taken a slightly different angle with its special events, which has more to do with political debate.

JQ: The spotlights were very important, but certain things run their course. I can't speak about internal decision-making at the festival because I'm not privy to it, but wasn't there a general sense that a single country can't produce enough good cinema on an annual basis to warrant a national spotlight every festival?

SF: I agree, it is a problem.

JQ: To return to cinematheques, it would seem a natural thing that film curators or programmers become festival directors, as you did, moving from the ICA in London to Rotterdam, though I think the positions involve very different talents. I would hate being a festival director – the politics, the administration, the diversion of attention from programming to many other areas in which I have no interest or competence.

How did you manage the change from programming a single space throughout the year, with the rhythms and concentration that entails, to a vast international festival, much less one held in a country in which you did not reside?

SF: I was very lucky in that Sandra den Hamer had a lot of experience, so I could concentrate on programming. The fact that we both became equal directors in due course reflected the importance of her contribution. What concerns me is the attitude that festivals can have general managers who are not cinephiles. That is not the case in Toronto or Rotterdam. It's a terrible idea to have a 'cultural manager' for a festival.

JQ: When you were at Rotterdam, was cinephilia or film knowledge a criterion for hiring people, even in areas such as administration or finance? Does it matter?

SF: It does, but I was not involved with hiring and firing. It was an interesting problem, that people would come up through the festival and want to do other things.

JQ: Everybody wants to be a programmer!

SF: Exactly, and they think they can do it, which explains the quality of some programmes.

JQ: Can we talk about models of curation? Some festivals, like Cannes or Venice, concentrate selection in the hands of one or two people, so one feels a consistent vision or taste at work. The New York Film Festival has a small committee, anchored by two or three permanents, and an equal number of rotating members.

SF: Don't get me started.

JQ: Others, like Toronto, really divvy up the programming into areas of interest and expertise, either by genre or geography, and try to maintain a kind of polyphony of many strong individual, curatorial voices. Which mode do you prefer? Rotterdam has a team of curators, less clearly defined in their purview than in Toronto. They seem to be all over the map, both metaphorically and actually. Which model do you think works best, or is it a festival-by-festival basis?

SF: This was always a discussion at Rotterdam because when I arrived there was this disconcerting obsession with Hubert Bals,[5] and how Bals supposedly saw all the films and judged them with his stomach, his gut reaction.

I always argued that the programming couldn't be done that way any more, because one person couldn't have the expertise in so many areas. It's important to work with people who have special knowledge. The role of the director is like organising a set of colours in a painting, and your individual curators or programmers are the colours. That said, there was a tendency for it to be all over the map because people would see films from different areas, though at that time I was the person who was doing basically all the Asian films.

JQ: Let's be honest. Any given year turns up ten, maybe twenty good-to-great films, if we're lucky. Yet as you point out festivals keep growing in size, show dozens, hundreds of films and make the case that each one is important or great or a masterpiece. Ideally, shouldn't every festival be a boutique festival like NYFF?

SF: It depends on what you think a festival is for. You can have the New York model which, aside from the avant-garde section, is designed to select the most important films of the year, with a certain coherency of taste. But then they end up showing many films – in what these days is a small festival – that will be theatrically released in coming weeks. The festivals that interest me are the ones that have a partisan approach, that emphasise certain kinds of cinema. At Rotterdam we tried through 'Filmmakers in Focus' to establish what the heart of the festival was along with the competition, but at the same time putting a wide range of cinema into the main programme, to take people places they normally would not go: to a gallery or make them look at Catherine Breillat or whatever, and you can do that only in a big festival. Though I have the ideal of a boutique festival, perhaps forty films or fewer, so that the audience can potentially see two-thirds of the programme, a family-sized festival a little like Telluride with an idea of progressive cinema. That's one idea of what a festival can be used as an educational tool. Some niche festivals, such as those concentrating on Asian cinema or a genre like science fiction, also aim to be informational, saying this is what's going on in that area, and the films don't have to be masterworks. But in the end I don't think the boutique festival is a good idea.

JQ: It's too limiting?

SF: Yes. And how many films in the New York Film Festival open three weeks later? That's an example of a festival which semi-takes its responsibility but is not polemical. I feel that there could be more space for making an argument about what someone has called 'a certain idea of cinema', pushing the boat out for certain films and approaches to filmmaking. New York does this, to a certain extent – but in a rather well-behaved Upper West Side sort of way.

JQ: The first time I met you, some fifteen years ago, you said over lunch that Toronto audiences were a bit high on themselves. What did you mean?

SF: I don't think I was being very fair.

JQ: Did being a festival director in the interim change your view?

SF: No, because some of the same thing is happening in Rotterdam. What I meant at the time was there is a way that is milked by the celebrity programmers. Someone introduced a film this morning: 'I am Noah Cowan's assistant.' Why we needed to know that, I'm not sure. I was being rather sarcastic back then about the way the Toronto audience had become rather self-congratulatory, which creates this buzz, because whatever they're shown, they love it. I was being unfair, and it's a great credit to the festival that they've built up this very enthusiastic and passionate audience. In Rotterdam, as the festival built, the audience also became very proud of being part of the festival, and that's a good thing but can become self-indulgent. It's promoted by Toronto with this 'we're the greatest festival in the world, you are the greatest audience in the world' mutual arse-licking that's not very attractive to watch.

JQ: Some festivals depend on general audiences, like Berlin and Toronto, both for income and excitement. It's a bit of a myth that Cannes is an industry-only festival – throngs of the general public get to go – but I think films still have their reputations made by the critics at Cannes, not so much by audience reaction. Do festivals that rely on audiences differ from those that don't, the way competitive festivals differ from ones that aren't? Does it skew the programming in any way?

SF: Rotterdam certainly had to take its audience into account. If you can get a very committed audience then in theory you should be able to take many more risks. You aim to persuade someone who can't get into a Todd Haynes film to see a Pedro Costa instead. My ideal of a festival-goer in Rotterdam was someone who would be trusting enough to take that risk. But we also have to talk about other publics, the international public, the critics, the filmmakers themselves.

JQ: Cannes programmes more for the critics than the public, and it occasionally puts difficult films in competition which often get hostile reactions from the critics.

SF: One of the terrible things about cinema is that it is simultaneously a business and industry and an art. There are enormous entanglements or confusions of criteria. For instance, in the UK, the traditional orientation of financial people is entirely towards the wider market and the more accessible film, and people no longer recognise the possibilities of visionary film or small-scale, small-audience work, whereas in the other arts, those possibilities are readily recognised. Let me give you an example of what we are seeing more and more in the trade papers – *Variety* and *Screen International*'s reaction to a young Japanese director's work, the idea that Naomi Kawase's films are slow and not going to be seen and therefore should be disregarded on those criteria.

JQ: There is the *Variety* polemic that comes out each year in Cannes that makes that very point: the cinephile world has become so hooked on Hou and Kiarostami, and the festival is not showing the cinema most of the world wants to see so what the hell are we all doing here?

SF: And not accepting that it's their job to make that gap closer, but the gap is actually getting much wider.

JQ: That polemic is made in *Variety* yet it still has some of the smartest film critics in the world, with great knowledge, and even within the constraints of *Variety*ese, they manage to write very well.

SF: That's absolutely true. Some are very cinephile, but they're often constrained to do very short reviews. It's very hard to make a coherent argument for auteur cinema if you're only reviewing the films one by one. *Screen International* is different in that regard.

JQ: Toronto has often been pushed to become a competitive festival, the argument being that it will never equal Cannes without a competition. Piers Handling has always resisted this, feeling that it would have a great distorting effect, that the festival would lose a lot of its sense of democracy, and there would be this undue attention on the competition. I'm very glad he has resisted.

SF: I agree. This issue of the value of competitions interests me because of course we have the Tiger awards in Rotterdam.

JQ: That feels like a very different kind of competition to me.

SF: Well, it is, it's part of the polemic. It's already worrying that Toronto is so obsessively emphasising its premieres. It's such bullshit, and the danger of a competition is that one has to insist on world international premieres.

JQ: The competition in Montreal is pathetic because it gets the scraps and leftovers from the other festivals.

SF: The same thing happens in San Sébastian, the competition is not very interesting, Karlovy Vary too. The fact is that Venice, Berlin, Cannes can scoop up the best films ... everybody wants to be in Cannes. Unless you have a different sort of competition, as a more polemical role like the one in Rotterdam.

JQ: Mannheim is another example. The year I was on the jury I was struck by how many strong films there were in competition that I had never heard of. They somehow managed to find a number of good small films that other festivals had ignored.

SF: And if you don't insist on premieres, you can actually have a good competition that draws attention to worthy films.

JQ: Will any festival ever overcome Cannes in international importance?

SF: I always thought of Rotterdam as on the second tier, below Cannes, Venice etc, and it's an interesting challenge as to where Rotterdam will go next. It's about six or seven in the world. I reject the notion of 'A' list festivals, because some of them...

JQ: Montreal. For fifteen years, I went to the Montreal World Film Festival and it was a case of rapidly diminishing returns. In the early years, it was the festival to go to see the European masters – Tarkovsky, Bresson, Olmi, Angelopoulos, Rohmer, Straub-Huillet – and such directors as Philippe Garrel, because believe it or not, Toronto wasn't showing them then. Slowly, as it lost ground to Toronto, it became major work to unearth what little treasure there was in Montreal.

SF: Toronto sucked the air out of all the Canadian festivals, didn't it? Not Vancouver, though, which is an interesting case of a festival with a strong Asian programme and is a public festival. Rotterdam is different than the other second-level festivals like San Sébastian and Karlovy Vary, because it managed to give itself a very particular niche role, which combined an adventurous public festival with something that attracts the industry. One of the questions Rotterdam has to face is: what are its priorities? Toronto does all these other things, Sprockets, the cinematheque. Is one dispersing one's energies by doing that? Festivals can diversify too much. In Rotterdam, energy is used up trying to do distribution, when it could be used to rethink how some sections of the festival should work. You ask about Rome and Venice, and it's quite clear how Toronto, since I first came, has earned major international status, and has become this essential meeting and market place as well as a popular festival. Berlin has become a more important market since Milan folded, but Venice will never really be able to have a market. Will Rome be able to get the films that Venice wanted and create a market around that? Venice has historical prestige, and Cannes as well, and you can't imagine it being pushed off its pedestal.

JQ: You can't imagine, to use the Rome/Venice analogy, Paris starting a festival in competition with Cannes. I think there should be a rule that film festivals can take place only in cities with few distractions, so one doesn't feel guilty watching films when one should be out in museums or sightseeing or at concerts ... which counts out Berlin and Venice for sure, but fits Rotterdam, mostly, and Cannes, totally.

SF: Paris would be an impossible place to have a festival, because there are films everywhere already. Generally you're right that festivals should be in anonymous cities with few distractions.

JQ: Festivals often push up against one another, the Montreal/Venice/Toronto/New York/Vancouver mash-up in the late summer and fall, for instance. Rotterdam almost always coincides with the Sundance film festival. Did Sundance cause problems for you – films that had to premiere there, or directors who couldn't make both festivals and chose Sundance? Or was Berlin more of a problem for Rotterdam?

SF: The problem with films and filmmakers was that often those who went to Sundance were dreaming of Cannes or Berlin and so would not commit to our programme. From the industry point of view it was tight and people quite often flew directly from one to the other. But it should be said that the taste of the two festivals didn't overlap so much. With Berlin, there the problem was much bigger because we were often chasing the same films and the 'Forum' and 'Panoram'a have under Dieter Kosslick become more and more insistent on premieres (to the detriment of the films at times, in my view. I understand now they won't even let some Hubert Bals Fund-funded films also be screened in Rotterdam if they want them). But speaking to one Rotterdammer recently, they had the view that Rotterdam often got things that Berlin wanted. We particularly tried to use the competition as a tool for that. Or in certain cases (Breillat), the 'Focus' also worked as a lever to get the premiere of a film (*Romance*) away from Berlin.

JQ: How does one assemble and structure a festival? There are too many sections in Rotterdam! Also in Toronto, I have to remind myself what the difference, say, between 'Visions' and 'Vanguard' is. I frankly can't figure out what the sections in Rotterdam connote, and it matters because they should be primarily serve as a guide through a voluminous selection.

SF: There are too many sections, and it's an internal problem at many festivals. We're dealing with this in Dubai. We have this section called 'The Cultural Bridge'. There are some bridges you can build in Dubai and some you can't, but it has been interesting to try to give some force to the idea of films bringing together various cultures.

JQ: Can you tell me what the restrictions are in choosing films for the Dubai festival, especially in terms of observing religious or cultural sensitivities?

SF: How does somebody who was in Rotterdam end up in Dubai, where apparently Peter Scarlet once said old festival directors come to die? I left Rotterdam, because both they and I thought it was time for a change, and because I wanted to become involved with production, but also wanted to stay in touch with programming. And if you're interested in a certain kind of cinema, you can see it only at festivals. So when I was offered programming at Dubai on a modest scale, I took it. There are cultural restraints. Homosexuality is not a subject that can be dealt with. The naked body, particularly of the female but also the male body, is not allowed. These are areas of 'cultural sensitivity'. But this is something that runs through a large number of countries, and in fact just twenty years ago, we should remind ourselves, was just as problematic in our countries. Now we're so awash with liberalism that we don't realise that England had very heavy censorship.

JQ: So did Ontario.

SF: Dubai's a very interesting context in which to adjust one's perspective. My heart is basically in the Rotterdam type of festival, and I am programming much more mainstream films in Dubai. But the festival becomes an interesting instrument, for the potential meeting of east and west, the Arab world with the rest of the world. There are several Arab festivals, but the area is crying out for a very official one that can actually attract industry, that can get the Arab filmmakers and producers to look at the wider world, a conduit or gateway. The more mainstream programming which is oriented to the public also helps to nurture Arab filmmaking. Importantly, half of the programme is devoted to new Arab cinema and this has a greater profile now with the beginning of competitions for Arab features, documentaries and shorts. The international section is designed to broaden the range of films seen in the UAE. Both sections are aimed not only at the Emirati audience but also at the very large international community present in Dubai. One of the constraints is having to respect the cultural mores and assumptions of the territory. To pretend one is in London and show only what one wants to show is just rather thoughtless.

JQ: That leads me to my Deborah Solomon question which is do you have qualms about working for an event that could be seen as cultural window dressing for a repressive regime?

SF: Yes.

JQ: That's it?

SF: (Laughs) I haven't finished. Do the people at the New York Film Festival have qualms about operating in a culture in which they have one of the most repressive presidents of all time? In Dubai, the role of the festival is indeed window dressing, yes. But here we come full circle from our discussion earlier about the role of film festivals all around the world. They are often a form of window dressing. But at the same time, maybe it's also a place where you can gradually shift the possibilities of what you can show and what can be seen. And this is something that is important for many Emiraties too.

JQ: Does your heart sink when you think a film will be perfect for Dubai suddenly has nudity?

SF: (Laughs) Yes. Sheila [Whitaker, a fellow programmer and one-time director of the London Film festival] and I are both very fond of describing that experience: 'Ah this is great, it's going so well—'

JQ: 'Oh no, there are some tits!'

SF: Tits could be okay, but full-scale bonking, or full frontal nudity are out.

JQ: So I take it that *Lust, Caution* will not be the opening film at Dubai this year.

SF: We're going to look at the edited-for-China version. Without the testicles.

JQ: There has been a lot of talk about the death of cinema, or in Susan Sontag's essay, the death of cinephilia, but something I'm concerned about is the *continuance* of cinema and cinephilia, but with a diminution in visual acuity, sensitivity – people seeing films on DVD and thinking they have seen and heard them; people not attuned to the differences between digital and analogue images and capabilities; people happy to watch images or films from any delivery system, no matter how small or downgraded. Cronenberg talked about this at Cannes this year – something about his daughter watching images from all kinds of sources, cell phones and such. I remember a panel at Rotterdam some years ago that was 'Cinema vs. DVD', and I was in the front row because I thought, 'oh finally, we're going to have this discussion', but it never happened because it was really an unquestioning celebration of DVDs, their educational possibilities, the democracy of film culture they create, but it was never broached what DVDs might do to people's sense of visual and aural acuity. Everything's compressed on them – you're not *hearing* the film. What role should film festivals play in advancing or preserving visual sensitivity? You and I feel very differently about digital – we've been having that debate for years – but I'm not talking just about digital.

SF: Should festivals have a stronger educational role? If you have a Resnais, a Michael Mann, a Costa or Diaz, and you're showing a plurality of cinema, how are you backing that up with ways to help people understand it? When I did the Ernie Gehr focus at Rotterdam, he started off doing the standard American-style Q&A – waiting for questions, and then he realised that a lot of people in the audience didn't have a clue about how to approach his films. I don't know what the answer to that is. There's the danger with a very plural festival that you'll never help people engage with that kind of cinema because you're too busy showing films. You can keep the gates, and put in the adventurous films, but you also need to help people understand the films. That's becoming more difficult because there's just this mass of stuff.

JQ: I can never trust my feelings about films when I see them at festivals.

SF: I think that's correct, because you're changing gear every hour and a half. The cinematheque experience is a different one. One ends up consuming film like a magpie at a festival.

JQ: Is it not worrisome that at a festival like Cannes where a film's reputation can be made or broken in one screening, and there are any number of factors that affect its reception? I think of some semi-disastrous press screenings, Victor Erice's *El Sol del Membrillo* and Pedro Costa's *Colossal Youth*, for instance. They both managed to recover after the festival, largely through the championship of some critics and programmers, but it is worrying that instant reputation is made in front of critics who are tired or hungry or cranky or have just been mishandled by a guard. We never talk about these issues, because to admit them is to suggest the process is very fallible.

SF: I don't know if I have spoken to the Cannes people about this problem, but there is always the question of whether you put a really tough film in competition, knowing that a portion of the press which is becoming lazier and lazier...

JQ: I attended the public screening of *Colossal Youth* and it was the opposite: totally respectful, totally quiet, few walkouts, prolonged applause.

SF: But the press – or portions of it – at Cannes sometimes can turn into a pack of ... ummmm...

JQ: Wolverines?

SF: Even someone like Hou Hsiao-hsien can suffer at Cannes, but if you're composing a competition, you *have* to put those films in. I think the other thing that is happening, and I don't know what we can do about it, is that many critics are becoming – or being pressured by their publications to become – much more consumer oriented, always asking whether a film will have a large audience. They're in danger of becoming tainted with an ideology that comes out of Hollywood: the idea that a film has to get the biggest possible audience is starting to shape everything. Poetry has no place in that approach.

Postscript: Rotterdam 2008

'I really like the films this festival supports', a young American director said to a critic from Cameroon the final frosty morn of the 2008 Rotterdam film festival. The critic murmured in reverential assent, needing no description of what the filmmaker meant: the small and wayward, the overlooked or neglected, the 'difficult or challenging', to use the boilerplate euphemisms for the kind of work Rotterdam has always championed. Perhaps I have lost patience with the bantam and undercrafted, but Rotterdam's traditional *parti pris* seemed a little pious and wearying in its latest edition. For every small discovery – such as Aditya Assarat's *Wonderful Town*, which went on to be the 'revelation' of the Berlin festival – there were endless stretches of digital dither, interchangeable studies of youth adrift, bored, alienated or (likely) all three, minor films from once-major directors, and Nice Little Movies that evanesced from the brainpan before their end credits. More memorable, but in the wrong way, was Yuya Ishii, hailed as the Next Big Thing with four features at the festival, all made in the last year, whose unspeakable puerility made one pine for Miike.

I heard more than once that the festival had lost its direction, though the Tiger Awards Competition featured its usual share of Rotterdam ready-mades, including critical favorite *The Sky, the Earth, and the Rain*, which won the FIPRESCI Award. Lovely and accomplished, José Luis Torres' sopho-more feature nevertheless sends troubling signals of the emergence of an international arthouse-festival formula, variant from film to film but adhering to an established set of aesthetic elements: *adagio* rhythms and oblique narrative; a tone of quietude and reticence, an aura of unexplained or un-earned anguish; attenuated takes, long tracking or panning shots, often of depopulated landscapes; prolonged hand-held follow shots of solo people walking; slow dollies to a window or open door framing nature; a materialist sound design; and a preponderance of Tarkovskian imagery. (Torres' film isn't quite the Tarkclone that Andrei Zvyagintsev's *The Banishment* is, but its aqueous world, tortoise-paced pans of entropic nature, and a studied composition of a suicidal girl in front of a lone, blasted tree all evoke the Russian master.) Has this uniform international aesthetic been nurtured by the festival circuit, and by such monetary bodies as Rotterdam's wholly admirable Hubert Bals Fund? And how can such films be considered discoveries when they conform to such a familiar style?

Rotterdam has always been celebrated as one of the last festivals that determinedly and successfully incorporates experimental and 'exploding' cinema into its programme. Such curators as Mark McElhatten and Edwin Carels have done a superb job over the years of ensuring that both experimental film and film-related art installations are intelligently presented. But why, after decades of experience, does Rotterdam so often seem technically inept in exhibiting this material, which only further marginalises it?: films shown in mirror reverse, silent works with sound turned up or accompanied by projectionists' voices booming from an ill-insulated booth, films shown out of focus. The technical ineptitude of the installation of Tsai Ming-liang's

The installation version of Tsai Ming Liang's *Is it a Dream?* screened at the 2008 Rotterdam Film Festival

recent film *Is It a Dream?* as part of the 'New Dragon Inns' sidebar was nothing short of scandalous. I had seen the work in its own mini-cinema at the
Venice Biennale, and though it was projected there on DVD, the image was
sharp, clear, precise (as was Wang Bing's 840-minute *Crude Oil* elsewhere
in 'New Dragon Inns'). In Rotterdam, the projection of the film was so
bleary, faces and objects were difficult to discern amid its swimming pixels.
To account for the blur, some argued that Tsai was entering a new phase of
visual abstraction, and one wonders how the director, whose only film this
was at Rotterdam, felt about the installation, especially given his opinion in
a *Daily Tiger* interview: 'I am not happy about the whole DVD medium, in
fact. The quality of film experience is crashing. People are now satisfied just
watching a film to find out what the story is. The experience is almost being
reduced to a kind of information gathering. What is going on? Who is it?
My films are really for the big screen only.'

Rotterdam's obsession with premieres, categorised according to angels-
on-a-pin divisions (world, international, European) and blazoned in the
festival's website, catalogue and daily newspaper, rendered Simon's comments

**Jacques Nolot's *Before I Forget* was one of the most noteworthy films screened at the 2008
Rotterdam Film Festival**

about Toronto's premiere fixation a little ironic. Just what did it mean to be a world premiere at Rotterdam, especially if the film were of little worth or consequence, and all the major movies came from previous festivals? Perhaps the accent on premieres accounted for Rotterdam's explosion into Toronto-like public success this year, with lineups and sell-outs the norm, not just for *Juno* or *No Country for Old Men*, but also for unknown, esoteric or historical work (such as Shelly Kraicer's important survey of Fourth Generation Chinese directors). The festival was still capable of providing exhilaration – a full house responding to a good, small film, such as *Munyurangabo*, that otherwise would probably never be shown in the Netherlands, for example – and of such serious undertakings as showing Jacques Nolot's superb *Before I Forget* in the context of its trilogy, with the Pialat-influenced *L'Arrière Pays* and outré *La Chatte a deux têtes*. But the prevailing tone of hype and hubris only added to the slow erosion of that old Rotterdam modesty, and I began to feel, much as the Huub Bals supporters did when Simon first transformed the festival from intimate to panoptic, nostalgic for its simpler self.

Notes (provided by Simon Field)

1 Sandra den Hamer started working with the festival in Huub Bals's period as director. She was Deputy Director when Simon Field became Director in 1997. In 2000 she joined him as a Director of the festival. When Simon Field left in 2004 she became sole director. She left the Festival in 2007 to become Director of the Nederlands Filmmuseum.

2 Kees Kasander is now best known as a producer, particularly of the films of Peter Greenaway. In 1996, he initiated the 'Exploding Cinema' section along with Femke Wolting when the festival was under the directorship of Emile Fallaux.

3 In 2003, when he was one of the 'Filmmakers in Focus', Guy Maddin presented the installation version of *Cowards Bend the Knee* at Rotterdam. Produced by The Power Plant, it was presented in Toronto in March–May 2003.

4 Among the 'Filmmakers in Focus' featured in Simon Field's years as director apart from those mentioned in the discussion were Alain Cavalier, Jang Sun Woo, Julio Bressane, Oshii Mamoru, Cipri and Maresco, Abolfazl Jalili, Kamal Hasaan, Stan Brakhage, Zacharias Kunuk and Jean-Claude Brisseau.

5   Hubert (or Huub) Bals was the legendary founder of the International Film Festival
    Rotterdam. He towered over its first twenty years and after his death in 1988 be-
    came something of a legend. For those interested in his life and a detailed history
    of those years when festivals were rather different creatures: see *Que Le Tigre
    Danse Huub Bals: A Biography* by Jan Heijs and Frans Westra. Otto Cramwinckel:
    Amsterdam 1996. The Hubert Bals Fund which supports the development and
    post-production of films from developing countries was named in his honour and
    memory.

Cinephilia and Film Festivals

ROBERT KOEHLER

Cinephilia non grata

It may be perverse to wish that something you write will be made irrelevant in the course of time, but that is exactly what I wish for the following thoughts. The central problem with film festivals in the Anglo-American world – the universe to which this book is mainly addressed – is not so much a willingness to show bad films. Though that is an issue. It isn't a paucity of films that connect with audiences, critics and the film community in general. Though this, too, can be a prickly matter. It isn't even a dependence on world premieres as part of the never-ending race between festivals to score points on the competition. On the face of it, not a problem at all, but in fact a matter that can actually be corrosive to a festival's health.

The most serious threat to the future of these festivals in these particular cultural climes, is another matter, seldom acknowledged in popular film journalism, in the trades, in industry accounts and (sadly) in cinema journals. It is their general and unexamined aversion to cinephilia, and an unwillingness to place cinephilia at the centre of festivals' activities. Look at any number of well-meaning festivals in the English-speaking world and a clear pattern is firmly in place. Just as the proverbial 'midnight madness'/'extreme visions'/'outer limits' (imagine your own trendy section title) is given a ghettoised place in the room – essentially at the kiddies' table while the adults are munching on the competition and premieres – any films and projects with explicitly cinephilic goals, if they're even given a slot at all, are usually either positioned at the outer fringes of the room, kept safely in the shadows or are placed in the festival's equivalent of Off-off-off Broadway. And this goes far beyond the mere creation of a cinephilic section, such as a revival of recently restored, once-lost film, or the recovery of the work representing a major if neglected career. The heart of the matter is an informed philosophy of cinephilia, a practice, an essential way of being and approach to cinema that either imbues a festival's programming, or doesn't. The construction and selection of any section immediately declares itself as, first of all, a critical statement, for film festival programming is always and forever in its first phase an act of criticism, and along with this a declaration of values, comprising two equally important components: those films that are included, and those films that are left out. Given that few festivals are ever able to generally secure the films they actually want (arguably only four – Cannes, Toronto, Venice, Berlin), and granted that international sales companies handling films now exert greater control over a film's travels than ever before (they are the new kingpins of festivals worldwide), a festival driven by serious cinephilia should still manage to get many of the films it wants on its radar. The question is if festivals in the Anglo-American world are primarily guided by these values, or simply use cinephilia as a sop, a sideshow, a marginalised event to please what they deem falsely to be a dwindling set of cinephiles.

This points to a first principle that, because it's also seldom acknowledged yet glaringly obvious, is also easily ignored: any festival that matters has only one crucial task, and that is to defend cinema. It should be obvious for no better reason than no other entity in the contemporary film world, including the ranks of film critics (who habitually as a group feel besieged and marginalised, even when they're not), is better equipped for such a defence. Given this, nothing else should come remotely close on the festival priority list. Not collecting a tasty basket of world premieres. Not enticing stars – meaning star directors, as much as star actors. Not appeasing sponsors (though sponsors are important, since they actually really do support the arts, and that is always and forever a good and beautiful thing). Certainly not satisfying the festival board of directors, who usually know little about cinema. All of these, some of them essential cogs in the festival machinery, can also be distractions from the central purpose of exploring new cinema, rediscovering old cinema and challenging the audience to encounter and wrestle with both. The moment of birth and history – these are the twin compass poles that should guide a festival and, by definition, a genuinely cinephilic one. Cinephilia operates with double vision: radar directed forward to the new, binoculars pointed back to the past. This would be a kind of perfect fusion – and is that ever really found? No, it's an act of finding history in the present moment, the encounter that finds Frederick S. Armitage's vertiginous and sensorial image explosions in 1903 to be more astonishing than any CGI and also finds that a new Raya Martin film can be transformative as it reverentially acknowledges silent film. In the past is the new, in the new the past, and the intersection is the friction that cinephilia requires – and that only a festival can provide in a living form with an audience. Forgetting this, or marginalising its import, turns festivals into ... into ... something else.

The self-made trap

What exactly? We can see it all around us, all the time, especially those of us – critics, programmers, filmgoers and the industry players who sell and buy films – who regularly attend festivals. I should be more exact in this case, and not call these other events 'festivals', even though that's the common term. Call them, instead, 'exhibitions'. In the North American world, these include Sundance, Toronto, South by Southwest, Seattle, Hamptons, Palm Springs and smaller, regional affairs ranging from Denver to Houston's Worldfest, as well as those hobbled dowagers stumbling along like Serge Losique's Montreal. They are generally well-funded and largely empty, generating considerable self-importance but only by a measure that gauges if the programmed films enter the distribution pipeline. (Some might add Tribeca, but Tribeca is too young, too nebulous to include in this group – albeit with the worrying signals that it may also become nothing more than an exhibition. Others might add New York, but that would be off the mark. The New York Film Festival is, simply, the New York Film Festival, and apparently always will be.) Seattle has been described as a kind of Wal-Mart of movies of any and all types that fit into some commercial category (non-commercial films being effectively banned from this massive six-week exhibition). South by Southwest has become a market for indie product, and not the place where the next Reg Harkema or Jake Mahaffy will be found. (On the contrary: Harkema told me that when he took his last film, *Monkey Warfare*, to South by Southwest, it was booked and scheduled with such glaring disregard and ineptitude that nobody knew the film was even there. It didn't help, as a side note, that Harkema is Canadian; South by Southwest is an unusually aggressive exhibition that privileges US filmmakers.)

And Sundance? Sundance has become, quite simply, a horror show for cinema: a place where more bad films can be seen under awful viewing conditions than any other festival, and yet which also paradoxically goes the extra mile to bother with a usually fascinating though small section for experimental and non- (or semi-) narrative film titled 'New Frontier' which is then scheduled in such a manner to ensure that as few people as possible will see it. The largest and most famous American film 'festival' has quite possibly damaged the cinema it was specifically designed to support – American indie film – more than any cluster of neglectful studios ever have, because it rejects cinephilia with cool (and in bad years, subfreezing) disinterest. Nothing better exemplified this in recent years than in 2004, when Ray Carney unveiled Cassavetes' nearly unseen original version of *Shadows* that Carney claimed (rather controversially) to have been found in some reel cans in the rear seat of a taxi. One might naturally assume that such a find would be first shown in the world's biggest event designed to celebrate independent film. Instead, Carney found friendlier hosts in Rotterdam, where *Shadows* screened to excited Dutch audiences. A long list of such American re-discoveries ignored by Sundance runs on and on; my favourite is how the festival, founded over two decades ago by Robert Redford, known for his devotion to Native American causes, failed to show the restored print of Kent MacKenzie's Los Angeles masterpiece, *The Exiles* – a film about young, aimless Native Americans in the city's old, virtually extinct Bunker Hill district and by light years the best American film ever made about Native Americans living in the modern world.

In purely cinephilic terms, these items amount to crimes. But that would be off the mark, since Sundance isn't about cinephilia; it's a stark example of what Quintín describes elsewhere in this volume as the recent phenomenon

Sundance passed on the restored version of Kent MacKenzie's acclaimed 1961 film, *The Exiles*

in which festivals have allowed themselves to become markets. Film markets, in and of themselves, are a necessary and fine thing, allowing the free
and rollicking exchange between buyers and sellers, sometimes in one of the
liveliest expressions of seat-of-the-pants capitalism this side of the Chicago
commodities exchanges. (Without these markets, stretching from Berlin to
Santa Monica, Cannes to Hong Kong, many foreign films would have otherwise floundered and never found their way to your city.) The markets, as
markets can often become, have proven so successful over the long term,
opening up countless doors to films that were previously shut out, that they
have proven too tempting to festivals that, by their nature, play a vitally
different game and serve a starkly different purpose. While the two animals
are indispensable to the overall international cinema world, they exist in
distinct systems that are better given as much separation as possible. The
success of one (markets), which is envied by the other (festivals), is merely
another phenomenon of ongoing globalisation processes, of which the cinema – despite the militant anti-globalisation objections of many filmmakers
and (judging by several comments in programme notes) programmers – is a

dramatic expression of its reality, power and potential. But as the Sundance experience demonstrates for the rest of the festival world, the effective over-throw of a festival's purposes by buyers and sellers chasing hot world pre-mieres is disastrous and corrosive to festival practice. Though a film's festival success can, and sometimes does, lead to market openings and prospects, the one shouldn't be allowed by the festival to bleed into the other. This, as any reader of many festival 'dailies' knows, is happily violated by some festivals as they regularly report on the sales of films in its programme. These be-come tacit admissions that the actual purpose of these exhibitions are sales markets under the culturally cool guise of a festival – marking the certain death of the festival as a whole, let alone the cinephilic festival.

The key issue in this regard is how Sundance has influenced other, small-er festivals to follow its practice of loading up with world premieres and as much English-language work as possible, at the expense of films from the vaster non-English world that challenge conventional cinema language and modes, as well as the large, wide and deep ocean of past, neglected films. This itch for world premieres can never seem to be completely scratched; I can't possibly count the number of North American directors and program-mers who, when asked to justify top-loading their programmes with world (or continental, or national, or regional) premieres, regardless of quality, don't resort to any fundamentally cinephilic explanations – which is at least sound, since there are none – but to extraneous yet financially relevant ex-planations. (1) Premiere-itis exists because festivals yearn to draw as much press as possible, and premiering films constitute news. (2) The closer a festi-val is to the major entertainment/media centres of New York and Los Ange-les (which means Tribeca, Hamptons, Woodstock, even SilverDocs in train-adjacent Maryland on one coast, and Los Angeles, AFI Fest, Palm Springs and Santa Barbara on the other), the greater the urge to lure entertainment and media power brokers and taste-makers. (3) Festivals claiming premieres get their name on the premiering film's publicity materials, constituting free advertising, translating in some crude respects into prestige. (4) The festival boards, particularly those in North America, tend to measure success partly on the metric of the number of premieres pulled off, and therefore pressure the director and programmers to come up with a sufficient quota of them for each edition, that quota varying from festival to festival. (5) The sheer presence and fact of premieres becomes a selling point in itself to the local and regional public which the festival is drawing from for its audience, as well as to the press. (6) Finally, if a bit more obscurely, festivals of a certain scale (and all of the above festivals qualify) have talked themselves into thinking that presenting world premieres guarantees a review in *Variety*, for which I regularly contribute as a critic and which adheres to an editorial policy of reviewing films on or as close as possible to the world premiere screening date.

All of these are, taken separately, reasonable enough when not put under the magnifying glass. But taken together, they form a trap – a self-made trap where many Anglo-American festivals currently are, even if they're unwilling to acknowledge it. Elsewhere in this volume, Mark Peranson refers to a 'mythical fifty' essential films that premiere somewhere in the world every year. It's one way of saying that, even in an excellent year (and we have been having several of late, as a matter of fact), there's always a finite number of new films that truly matter, new work that's essential to see if you consider yourself a viewer of the most vital contemporary cinema. I would say that a year with more than sixty is extraordinary, and that under forty is closer to the norm. Moreover, this circle of films with few exceptions premieres in an elite group of festivals, led by Cannes and Venice, followed by Toronto, Vienna and Rotterdam, then by Berlin, then by Locarno. This is open to quibbling; some wouldn't include Vienna or Locarno, since they perceive both as too off the mainstream – but they would be wrong; others might eliminate Rotterdam, since the trendy view is to deem that it's best days are behind it – but that's much too short-sighted. Some critics, as well, are ready to blast Berlin's behemoth festival into outer space, with the hope that it will never return to Earth.[1] One can't honestly include Sundance in this group, which only rarely has something along the lines of Lance Hammer's *Ballast*, key American films that are also key films. Besides, Sundance, for all its muscle to lay claim to premiering American indie films, increasingly has competition in the US as a launch pad for films of national (and possibly international) import, from Tribeca to South by Southwest to burgeoning Cinevegas, which happens to be run by Trevor Groth who also serves as a senior Sundance programmer and regularly manages to score as many or more artistically crucial films in any one year as the Monster from Park City, and on a tiny fraction of its budget and in a much more compressed calendar. The essential point in all of this is that there are only so many crucial and necessary films to go around, and smaller festivals assuming that they can premiere important or even just quality films are generally deluding themselves. What they're doing instead is showcasing dressed-up mediocrities that are here today, gone tomorrow.

This, to put it mildly, does not defend cinema. If festivals in the English-speaking world are interested in not driving themselves into a position in which they become marginalised for just about every conceivable kind of audience – and in the Anglo world, there are too many kinds to count, if judged by the proliferation of micro and niche festivals catering to every conceivable taste, from gay-lesbian to indie scenesters and across the ethnic rainbow – they would do well to study those festivals that retain and deepen their strains of cinephilia with each edition. There's no good reason to simply duplicate their examples down to the details; after all, festivals as various as Amiens, PIA and BAFICI developed their own points of view on cinephilia, views that reflect the tremendous range of approaches that critical programming can take (all programming under the guise of cinephilia is criticism by other means). At the same time, while avoiding dumbed-down copycatting, the universe of festivals that has tended to avoid cinephilia or marginalise it out of some mistaken notion that such an approach proscribes the audience (which is to say, out of fear) can usefully study why cinephilic festivals succeed, and why they have become to be seen as crucial to film culture. The logic is simple: distinctive festivals have immeasurably value-added qualities, whereas festivals developed to mimic their big brother events inevitably see their value diminish in line with their similarity to each other.

Festivals with voices

Given all the above, it would be wrong to leave the impression that there are no cinephilic festivals in the Anglo world. In North America, look no further than Vancouver and Telluride for two utterly distinct festivals, ones that indefatigably possess particular voices. Vancouver's stems from its unique geographic-cultural position, in a city perched on the very southwest corner of Canada, able to gaze at a sober distance across the vast expanse of its own country (and far from the madding crowds and noise of the Toronto-Quebec-Ottawa corridor that tends to dominate so much of Canadian culture) while looking east to Asia as a key Pacific Rim city. With the 'Dragons & Tigers' section (including its 16-year-old competition of new work by young Asian filmmakers) forged by programmer-critic Tony Rayns (and now co-programmed by critic and Chinese cinema expert Shelly Kraicer), Vancouver has been able to build a section without peer and parallel outside of Asia itself. The visitor to Vancouver will immediately note the unabashed radical nature of many of the 'Dragons & Tigers' films: recent winners such as John Torres' *Todo Todo Teros*, Robin Weng's *Fujian Blue* and Zhang Yuedong's *Mid-Afternoon Barks* attest to this. The selection is guided by a generally rigorous concern for new forms of cinematic expression; that is, work that extends and tests the boundaries of what's possible within cinema, all underlying a programming philosophy (generally extending in principle to the larger festival) that never betrays a concern for appeasing audiences – a key point and one that Anglo festivals must take to heart. Just as key is this: the audience, almost entirely local, shows up, frequently in droves, and for the whole range of work, whether it's the Western unveiling of Bong Joon-ho's *Memories of Murder* or the Korean documentaries of Zero Chou and Hoho Liu. This kind of commitment – and the results – helps Vancouver stand out not just from the Canadian fall festival circuit (Montreal, Toronto, Atlantic), but also from the rest of the continent. It's instructive to consider, for example, that no generalist North American and Anglo festival has picked up on the 'Dragons & Tigers' idea and created a similar programme/competition with a focus on other zones such as Latin America or Eastern Europe, two areas bursting with interesting new cinema.

Telluride may not be news to many, given the lavish coverage it steadily receives in the mainstream American press.[2] But its position as a fall festival launching pad by mini-major studios and quasi-independent distributors for their awards season product line – the ongoing scourge of North American and UK fall festivals from Toronto to London – has managed, through no fault of the festival but entirely through the fault of many of the American critics covering it, to distract from its important role as a presenter of archival discoveries of the most rarified kind. The efforts and victories in presenting the widest possible range of archival discoveries must be regarded as an essential contribution to world cinephilia. One example among many is Tom Luddy's hunt for and discovery in Moscow of the extant print of Mikhail Kalatozov's *I Am Cuba*, shown at Telluride before it became a durable legend as the strangest and most Gothic cultural example of the odd and inevitably doomed Cuban-Soviet collaboration of the 1960s.[3] Another is certainly the now-legendary 1998 screening of the best possible existing 'version' by Rick Schmidlin of Erich Von Stroheim's *Greed*.[4] And much as *I Am Cuba* has gone on to enjoy a healthy life in, first, video and then DVD, other Telluride recovery projects of immense importance have been widely screened and distributed, led by Abel Gance's *Napoleon*. The Telluride example, joined by Pordenone, demonstrates that silent films, when presented with the proper amount of élan and event status, can have a vital life with contemporary audiences. Indeed, part of the ongoing cinephilic success of festivals like Telluride and Pordenone with their abiding concern for silent cinema (as well as the work of major film archives) is partly due to the commercial market that the DVD format has created for older silent and early sound films.

And speaking of Pordenone's Giornate del cinema muto ... as a silent nirvana, it's the paragon of a festival with a voice. The fact that it has a mission, to present the latest finds in silent cinephilia, is in part what distinguishes it. Telluride pulls together some of its programming from Pordenone's work (currently run by David Robinson), though it remains an unanswered oddity that Telluride should remain just about the only major Anglo-American festival to sustain such dedication, and that others don't simply piggyback onto the Pordenone bandwagon – not, in itself, a difficult thing to do. In the UK, for instance, there are outposts such as the British Silent Cinema festival in Nottingham, but its programming – frequently in collaboration with the BFI – is strictly national in scope. The Pordenone model, by contrast, is aggressively global.

The other lesson of Pordenone to other festivals: find an unexplored pocket – or, in this case, chasm – of cinema, and seek to become dedicated to it. One of two key premises of festival cinephilia is that our current knowledge of films and filmmakers is growing but still limited; that there remain numerous filmmakers, actors, technicians and countries in which archival study and awareness have only started to produce results. (The other premise is that there's much recent and contemporary cinema to discover.)

By burrowing into the three-plus decades of silent film, where so much remains to be found and seen, Pordenone has been instrumental in the general rediscovery process that defines this wing of cinephilia.[5] One aspect of this is historical, and actually biographical. For several years running, the festival's 'The Griffith Project' has surveyed D. W. Griffith's career, but in a novel way: instead of organising by theme or style, each year of Griffith's career is looked at in separate chronological blocks of time. (The 2007 edition, for instance, surveyed years 1921–24.) Selections from major archives and studios are regularly profiled, to underline the basic truth that a local archive or production house is often the most likely source – and restorer – for the work of that nation's filmmakers; the Danish Film Institute's magnificent efforts in the cause of Dreyer is a truly glorious instance of this, and Shochiku's archiving and restoration of 33 of Ozu's films during the 2003 centennial celebration demonstrates how the rediscovery-restoration project can extend beyond archives to producing studios – a lesson that's been seriously taken to heart in Hollywood by only one major studio, and that would be Sony.

History, with a difference

Pordenone shows that there's more than one way of teaching film history to audiences. Yet just as exciting as the Pordenone model are other festival projects that work to understand the depths of filmmaking careers and the companies that produced them. The former had, for some time, been a specialty of Rotterdam: pick a handful of interesting filmmakers, and put their opus on screen. My first year at Rotterdam turned out to be a case in which I was completely distracted from the new films and drawn to the flames of Raúl Ruiz, Ken Jacobs, Isaac Julien and Tunde Kelani – with very few exceptions, filmmakers who had been routinely ignored by US festivals.[6] Such concentrated programmes, though difficult to manage inside the hubbub of a festival, effectively force the viewer into a state of total absorption: you will see the body of work, and you will see it now. (Because it'll be gone tomorrow.) As a concept, the Rotterdam model of career cinephilia is simplicity itself – which doesn't diminish the fact that organising it is anything but simple.

So it's an interesting but mysterious fact of the current festival circuit that North American viewers must now travel to Mexico City or Buenos Aires if they'd rather not cross the Atlantic or Pacific to visit other festivals with careerist programming ambitions. BAFICI (or as it used to be officially known, the Buenos Aires International Festival of Independent Cinema) is covered in depth and with a unique personal perspective elsewhere in this volume by former director Quintín. But it's worth emphasising the festival's astonishing devotion to career surveys as a cinephilic pathway, particularly if it's viewed as a means of telling film history from a critical perspective. (BAFICI has been run since the Quintín era by film critics, a species whom most Anglo-American festivals are content to let loose during the actual festival run but would never in a million years be allowed to actually be in charge.) The selected careers include the dead (Hugo Fregonese, Frank Zappa) and the living, often superb, frequently neglected filmmakers, or filmmakers whose work is just beginning to be felt on the world scene, even though they may have already made several films; recent notable non-dead cases include Pere Portabella, Jem Cohen, Luc Moullet, Peter Whitehead, Yervant Gianikian and Angela Ricci Lucchi, Nicolas Klotz and Kobayashi Masahiro. Not only does BAFICI programme up to as many as fifteen career surveys per edition – that would be roughly fourteen more per annum than most festivals in the world consider doing – but they're done comprehensively; this means, in the case of Whitehead, including nearly a dozen clips and promo shorts he made during his fecund 1960s period, as well as his seminal swinging London films and beyond – in other words, the complete works.

In Mexico City, FICCO (Mexico City International Contemporary Film Festival) emerged five years ago as a fresh cinephile outpost in a country badly in need of one since, up until then, the long-running Guadalajara festival had had to service every kind of imaginable constituency as the key platform for new Mexican film production, from the buyers and sellers at the festival's thriving market, to visiting critics and local audiences. FICCO did precisely what no North American festival has done before or since, which is to follow the BAFICI model and to adapt it to local circumstances. Flagrantly international and non-Mexican in its focus (though with a fascinating component for new Mexican digital production, the site of most of the country's most exciting work), FICCO delves into careers with BA-FICI's brand of comprehensive seriousness. A recent survey of the complete work of Maurice Pialat is a typical case, allowing the North American visitor just about the first opportunity outside of France to explore what's arguably the most rewarding oeuvre in recent French film history, and one that, in retrospect, is without imitators. An important aspect of the career studies in both BAFICI and FICCO are the introductory (and bilingual) essays included in the festivals' generously thick catalogues, usually written by critic-programmers with great sensitivity and depth, as well as brevity.[7] These essays are also an extension of a larger project carried on by many non-Anglo-American festivals – namely, book publication. Locarno, for example, publishes volumes in conjunction with *Cahiers du Cinéma*, while BAFICI usually issues two volumes per festival edition (one on a particular filmmaker, another on a tendency in that year's programming).[8] For the cinephilic festival, such publishing is a routine matter, an understood part of what goes into the festival's content – as essential to the festival as the films or panel discussion. These books extend the festival's cinephilia in two ways: first, as a permanent record of a topic explored in the festival's edition and as a means of furthering film history by a non-academic route, and second, as a way to reinforce the idea that festivals are affairs in criticism.

A fine example that combines publication with exploring film history, with a difference, is the Amiens film festival. Since there are countless ways of telling history – and since history is made by the historians – Amiens, under the creative direction of Jean-Pierre Garcia, devotes a portion of its programming to a global tour of, as their literature terms it, the great studios of the world. The most recent study centered on Nikkatsu Studio, home at one time or another to such disparate filmmakers as Mizoguchi Kenji and Suzuki Seijun. Garcia has organised past overviews of a range of studios from Babelsberg, Churubusco and the Shaw Brothers to Hammer Films and Armenia's Armenfilms, while, looking forward, he's planning a study of a Mumbai studio. In each case, an accompanying book, typically around a hundred pages, fleshes out the background and provides further critical study into the selected studio films.[9] No other festival, to my knowledge, surveys film history from such an angle.

Festival cinephilia now

Festival cinephilia for new work has been largely misunderstood, certainly in North American circles, where the post-summer pressures to play awards season films, as well as the increasing power wielded by sales companies to screen their new slates, tends to overwhelm the sensibilities of even the most acute and intelligent programmers. It hardly helps when the trades deliver a resounding vote of no-confidence to those festivals which are bound and determined to explore the far reaches of new cinema, whether it be in Locarno, Vienna, BAFICI, PIA, Rotterdam or Vancouver.[10] A programming philosophy based on aesthetic selection amounts to an argument for a certain kind of cinema that may run counter to what's perceived as 'commercial' (a term so loosely and frivolously used that it's ceased to have meaning), but which generates a larger and more generous art form. The developing acceptance in Western festivals of the recent Filipino film movement provides an especially gratifying illustration of how festivals, their cultural antennae built to take in signals from long distances, are able to affect filmmaking practice. It's by now widely accepted that without Rotterdam's Hubert Bals Fund and its mission to fund and support film artists in the 'Third' and developing worlds, a significant number in the global 'margins' would have been unable to make films at all, and the case of the Philippines – I especially have in mind Lav Diaz, Raya Martin, Khavn, John Torres and Brillante Mendoza – would have been one of dashed hopes. There's no doubt that the sheer radical libertarianism of film practice, in which these young directors make any kind of film at all, using any means at their disposal, free of government support (since there's none to offer in the first place, which has turned out to be their blessing), would have still resulted in an astonishing flow of films. But with Rotterdam, Vienna, BAFICI and Vancouver being particularly instrumental as early adopters of the new Filipino cinema (with Toronto as a special case, exhibiting Lav Diaz), I'd argue that this is a particular test-case for contemporary cinephilia: finding radical new work that punches holes through the walls of cinema's supposed peripheral limits, and then taking the brave decision to show it to audiences. Only with such an act, a necessary one that's steadily showered with cat-calls and derision from various corners of the industry and press – not including those corners blissfully ignorant that such movements of new cinema exist at all – is contemporary cinema able to exist. The pressures against this work are palpable in the English-speaking world only because the festivals located there have failed to develop their audiences for the films. The only means by which Pedro Costa's filmography was finally able to be theatrically presented in major North American cities was in a touring show in 2007, after most significant festivals on the continent had failed to screen even one of his features, including *Colossal Youth*. This repeated a similar pattern that previously applied to Abbas Kiarostami and Hou Hsiao-hsien: only with touring career retrospectives were their films finally shown, in most cases long after they had screened in cinephilic festivals. That these touring shows draw considerable crowds – and they have, consistently, throughout the continent – definitively proves the short-sightedness of festivals failing to learn from festivals with adventurous programming. Or let's put this another way: there was a day in Mexico City when films like Hugo Vieira Da Silva's *Body Rice* or Pere Portabella's *Die Stille vor Bach* might not have had a chance to screen at all, not even at the city's respected Cineteca. But with an audience still being developed by FICCO for such remarkable pieces of new cinema, the opportunity now exists, and a fresh outpost for cinema's future has been established. The opportunity awaits for the next festival to step up, and take the chance.

Notes

1   Sundance is hardly the only major festival that has been critically examined and found seriously wanting, as I sought to explain in my analysis of the 2008 edition. ('All Bushed Out', *Cinema Scope*, Spring 2008, Issue 34, 56-59) Olaf Möller also delivered perhaps the toughest and most thoroughgoing of several attacks on Berlin 2008, when he noted that 'it seems as if those responsible for the Berlinale dream of a festival without films: just celebrities, the industry and a handful of good intentions, without any pesky movies distracting attention, posing awkward questions, and generally causing trouble.' (See Möller, 'Lowering the Bar', *Film Comment*, May–June 2008, Volume 44, Issue 3, 56-59)

2   For the sort of overview typical in the middlebrow press, see the chapter 'Telluride' in Kenneth Turan (2002) *Sundance to Sarajevo: Film Festivals and the World They Made*. Berkeley: University of California Press. At least, Turan's extremely flawed

and thinly conceived exploration of world festivals groups Telluride with Pordenone, another small-scaled festival with a single-minded commitment to silent film. But Turan's chapter and annual Telluride reports for the *Los Angeles Times* typically relegate the genuinely cinephilic discoveries at Telluride to the bottom of his stories, with the lead weighted toward high-profile fall awards season releases. A similar pattern can be seen at work in Roger Ebert's Telluride reports, with major cinephile events commonly given passing mention, or provided as colour to dress up the main thrust of the story, which is describing Telluride as a platform/launchpad for the fall season. This effectively distorts Telluride's place in cinephilia, while disguising the distortion. For a telling example, see Ebert (2004) 'Telluride: Three Very Different Looks at Sex', *Chicago Sun-Times*, http://rogerebert.suntimes.com/apps/pbcs.dll/article?AID=/20040906/FILMFESTIVALS02/409060301: Accessed 1 April, 2008.

3   The work involved in rescuing the film from obscurity has been obscured itself, in part due to the abysmal failure of filmmaker Vicente Ferraz to credit Luddy and his detective work in his documentary, 'The Siberian Mammoth', on the making of *I Am Cuba*.

4   I place the term 'version' in quotes only because a good deal of Schmidlin's painstaking work featured the careful selection of stills to stand in for missing footage.

5   Jay Weissberg's detailed overview of Pordenone's 2003 edition for *Senses of Cinema* is illustrative, devoting considerable space to the festival's survey of the career of Russian actor Ivan Mosjoukine (a.k.a. Mozhukhin). See http://www.sensesofcinema.com/contents/festivals/03/29/22nd_pordenone.html Accessed: 20 March, 2008.

6   As with so many other aspects of cinephilia in the US and Canada – and to a certain degree in the UK, Ireland and Australia – the heavy lifting of putting together career retrospectives typically falls to well-endowed cinematheques and archives. This was true in the specific case of Ruiz, who was given a modest touring retrospective over a decade-and-a-half ago that I saw at the UCLA Film and Television Archive.

7   There are several fine examples, making it difficult to select just one, so I'll mention two. See 'Juguetes peligrosos' by Javier Porta Fouz and Diego Trerotola for a fine summa on the strange career of Oku Shutaro, in the catalogue for the ninth edition of BAFICI. See also 'La esencia de la realidad' by Jorge Garcia for as excellent a brief overview of Pialat's work as can be found in any language, in the catalogue for the fifth edition of FICCO.

8   Or, such as in the case of a new 2008 book on Jose Luis Guerin, a platform to launch the book. Carlos Losilla and Jaime Pena, eds., *Algunos paseos por la ciu-*

dad de Sylvia: Un cuaderno de notas. Buenos Aires and Gijon: Buenos Aires Independent International Film Festival and Gijon International Film Festival, 2008. This was one of two books co-published or solely published by BAFICI in advance of its 2008 edition, a practice that the festival has maintained since close to its founding in 1998.

9 Fabien Gaffez, ed., *Sous le soleil de Nikkatsu.* Amiens: Festival international du film d'Amiens, 2008.

10 For one instance among many, see Derek Elley (2007) '60th Locarno fest witnesses "Rebirth"', http://www.variety.com/article/VR1117970101.html?categoryid=13&cs=1 Accessed: 1 May, 2008.

Here and Elsewhere: The View from Australia

ADRIAN MARTIN

The first film festival I travelled far abroad to see was Rotterdam in 1997. I was a late starter at this game: 37 years old, and already a film critic for twenty years. For me, that edition of Rotterdam was a complete eye-opener, and a fulfilment of most of my cinephilic dreams: sitting in a front row inches from one of my heroes, Werner Schroeter, as he unfussily stood up to introduce his avant-garde opera film *Love's Debris* (1996), was merely the cream on the cake of everything I was able to guzzle off the various screens (cinematic, televisual, museum and gallery) available that year.

I was there from before the first screening to after the last screening (something that – I would realise later – few professional critics actually do). But on that final day, reading the daily newspaper published by the festival, I received a rude shock: a 'people's choice' listing, based on the polling of the event's audiences, ordered from one to one hundred. The luckless title right down the bottom was a film I adored, and had critically defended (for, back in my country, it was briefly in danger of being altogether censored): David Cronenberg's *Crash* (1996). And the film on top was one of the kind that, in my mind, I had fled precisely in order to come to Rotterdam: the disgustingly middlebrow, sentimental, 'true life', made-in-Australia hit *Shine* (1996). This was a 'disconnect', a true moment of dissociation that alerted me to the difference – alas, even in the Rotterdam of my dreams! – between the cinephile audience (which longed to stamp its taste on the entire event) and the 'normal'

'de Doelen', headquarters for the Rotterdam Film Festival

audience for this, and possibly almost every, film festival. And the normal audience in this case was, no doubt, comprised mainly of Dutch locals.

Those who are lucky or rich enough to be professional Film Festival-goers – whether as journalists, critics, programmers or film distributors – occasionally need to recall a time in their lives before they had the chance to travel internationally. For me, this recollection is easy: I have a vivid sense of what it once was to be a relatively home-bound local (since I remained one for an unnaturally long time), waiting for the Melbourne film festival to roll out its offerings each year.

This is a poignant (as well as exciting) situation which, I suspect, is at the origin of the cinephile passion for many people in many countries: the film festival is what – well beyond newspapers or magazines, radio or television, telephone or computer – gives the non-traveller his or her glimpse of a wide, rich world, so full of different sensibilities, visions and stories. The longing for world cinema stirred in this heady situation is, for a sedentary viewer, simultaneously a longing for the world itself. It is akin to the image of the melancholic young dweller of a small country town in Jacques Brel's song

'Mon enfance' who gazes wistfully – exactly like, 34 years later, the characters of Jia Zhangke's *Platform* (2000) – at the train that is slicing its way across the landscape to unseen territories beyond, the 'train I have never caught'.

It is easy to overlook the reality that for many members – sometimes a majority – of a festival audience, the experience is local (and special) in just this sense. When seasoned critics and other well-travelled festival observers express (as they almost invariably do) their weariness or bitter disappointment at seeing, say, *The Five Obstructions* (2003) or the latest Claude Chabrol movie pop up at yet another event on their global itinerary, they overlook the fact that, for a sizeable number in the crowd, this may well be their one and only chance to see that film on a big screen, and in the company of like-minded others.

Festivals that contain this thrill of local experience are still with us; but what has, for the most part, vanished in many places are festivals that are *only* local, and tailored specifically to the characteristics of such a (usually grateful) reception of world cinema. A note of nostalgia inevitably creeps into discussion of these matters, as critic-programmer-historian Bruce Hodsdon noted in his account of the 2007 Brisbane film festival: 'comparisons are often made between the film festivals [of the 1960s] and contemporary festivals, to the latter's detriment'. Hodsdon evokes the days when festivals were 'less complex beasts', more contained in their programming and based on a stable community experience:

> … a subscriber became part of what was in essence a captive audience. Once the decision was made to become a subscriber it was quite feasible to see every film on the programme at no additional cost. At the 1968 Sydney Film Festival (SFF), for example, there were a total of 28 sessions over 13 days on a single screen, less than one-tenth of the sessions and films screened at the SFF in 2007. Of the 26 features, 20 were of European or Soviet origin with a single feature length documentary in the programme. There was a greater sense of shared experience – a community of festival-goers in cinemas accommodating up to 2000 or more for a series of single screenings open simultaneously to all subscribers.[1]

Nostalgia aside, what we are witnessing today is not merely the existence of two separate, very different audiences or constituencies (local and itinerant) attending film festivals, but the increasing gap between two kinds of Festivals

– or two kinds of festivals within the one festival. There are festivals that play to a home audience, and festivals that play to an international audience, a crowd of visitors with specialist interests (whether cultural or commercial or both) in global film culture – and now, festivals that try to play to both audiences at once, via the differential 'streaming' of its programme content.

To put it another way: many festivals now aspire – to the material and cultural extent that they can – to be like the major event of this kind on the film world's calendar, namely Cannes. And however one might choose to describe Cannes, its nature is determined by the fact that it is absolutely *not* a local festival: its programme is not in any sense intended for or directed at inhabitants of the French Riviera. It is the very model of a cosmopolitan, international arts event that may be 'hosted' by a particular city or community, but whose entire audience is transported in from beyond it.

This quality of statelessness that is characteristic (to varying degrees) of many modern festivals is both a commercial situation (festival as marketplace, both for distributors buying films and filmmakers hoping to raise finance on projects), and a social experience (festival as jet-setting lifestyle) which can be deeply attractive (and even addictive) to those who taste it. When the Buenos Aires festival (known as BAFICI), for example, in the early years of the new century, declared itself semi-officially to be a 'festival for critics', it was consciously styling itself as a more intellectual and avant-garde, but no less cosmopolitan, version of Cannes. But this plan or dream – as history has shown – often conflicts with other agendas driving festivals, especially those we might label national or nationalist: a festival as showcase for national production for the local audience and industry, as well as for any important or influential visitors from abroad. This tension has been evident, for instance, in the history of the Rotterdam festival over the past decade: the appointment of Simon Field as its Director for eight years was a triumph for cultural cosmopolitanism of a cutting-edge type, but led to unrest among those who felt that the event's local character as a festival by and for the Dutch was slipping away or being swiftly marginalised.

Of course, festivals around the world have tended inexorably to fragment in other ways and directions as well, further detonating the once-upon-a-time 'local community' experience. In the place of the small, focused event of old, the contemporary festival (as Hodsdon notes) 'is now a segmented programme spread across a number of venues aimed more often than not at niche audiences'.[2] We are all familiar with what this means in practice: there is a stream of Asian genre films for their devoted fans; comfortable comedy-dramas of middle-class life set in exotic locales for the more mainstream crowd; documentaries (usually either about politics or music) for those who prefer a bigger-than-TV non-fiction experience; and token sidebars of experimental cinema, animation, short films, dance films, whatever...

The cinephile can welcome and enjoy this sort of fragmentation – for the individual, it increases the delirious range of choices at the largest 'smorgasbord' festivals, after all – but also, inevitably, enters into battle with it. What happened to the festival as a 'film culture' event, as an opportunity for mass pedagogy? The niche-oriented festival merely confirms spectators – or rather, gangs of spectators – in the already-established prison-house of their frequently rigid, exclusive tastes; as a general rule, audience members who follow the marketing cues designed precisely to 'target' them do not wander over and cross the lines of starkly diverse types of cinema. Where can the fervent dream of cinema as transformative experience – which is, from a certain angle, the very heart of the cinephile passion, and cinephile culture – go in this kind of segregated landscape? Jean-Marie Straub and Danièle Huillet may have (as Australian legend has it) looked aghast upon the photo of the interior of the enormous State Theatre when the then-Director of the Sydney film festival showed it to them, inadvertently inciting their demand that their films play in a much smaller and more 'just' space – but, still today, cinephiles tend to swoon at the thought of vast picture palaces (even of the contemporary multiplex variety) filling up with mass bodies curious to taste an Abbas Kiarostami, Béla Tarr, Chantal Akerman or James Benning.

It is fascinating, today, to look back at two major Australian think-pieces of the early 1980s that reflected on these difficult issues of what film festivals are, have been, and should be – and began the kind of institutional study of festivals that has only recently come back onto the university cinema studies agenda. Unlike most festival reviews or reports – there is surely no genre of film criticism that is more ephemeral, or of less 'general interest', save to those who were themselves there, or who have a professional stake in monitoring their reception[3] – 'The Triumph of Taste', written by Kathe

Boehringer and Stephen Crofts in 1980, is a wide-ranging critique of a certain kind of festival dominant in that period.[4] To them, the Sydney film festival typifies the consumerist spectacle of a comfortable, unchallenging humanism. Festivals have always been praised for their efforts (explicit or incidental) that have aided the cause of multiculturalism, but such a show can readily become a sham when all the world's diverse cultures are ground down and homogenised into the one, universal 'human spirit' story of suffering, resilience, triumph, hope... The entire apparatus of a film festival exists, in this sense, to simultaneously present cultural difference (the 'window on the world' line so popular in festival promotion) and erase it. The lack of (in many cases) any extensive background contextual information on the films – via notes, essays, introductions, in-depth seminars, and the like – aggravates this myopia. All we get (in the immortal words of this piece) is:

> ... the Anglo-Saxon Film Critical Newspeak of hand-me-down literary critical discourse peppered with tasteful superlatives and silvertail art-amateur clichés [...] infinite permutations of beautifully/handsomely/flawlessly/faultlessly/superbly/sumptuously made/rendered/realised/executed/handled-photographed/acted.[5]

What, in this account, has changed today? On the one hand, the multicultural 'world cinema' package has – married to the soundtrack of the similar phenomenon of 'world music' at its most superficial – largely moved from the big screens of festivals to the little screens of subscription TV (such as Australia's 'World Movies' channel) and DVD. On another hand, turning to the standard films which, in 1980, greased the wheels of complacent multiculturalism, Boehringer and Crofts give the 'cosmopolitan vs local' conflict a particular, and today surprising, inflection: for them, the films expressly made for the then-burgeoning international art film market (such as Volker Schlöndorff's *The Tin Drum*, 1979) are not *local* films at all, not made for (or arising from) what the Australian film critic John Hinde once called the 'seminal' audience of any given nation.[6] They are stateless, rootless films, and damned as such by Boehringer and Crofts: a strange judgement to re-encounter in a time when the work of Olivier Assayas, or the recent forays of Hou Hsiao-hsien into Japan or France, are praised precisely for their speedy, moody, 'border crossing' cosmopolitanism.

The second notable article from the archives of Australian film criticism is by Lesley Stern, discussing the Melbourne film festival of 1981.[7] Like Boehringer and Crofts, Stern finds the facile sorting of films by country, genre or auteur unengaging; she calls for a more suggestive grouping or *networking* of the films – of the kind actualised in a merry rhizomatic map handed out to the public of the Ljubljana film festival in 2007. Stern calls this mode of (hopeful) experience 'the festival as a moveable feast'; she makes great play with culinary and digestive metaphors, trying to salvage the image of a festival as an all-over smorgasbord, thus turning the pessimistic Debordian critique of the festival as 'spectacle of consumption' into a perversely enjoyable 'consumptive spectacle' – one in which the excess and slippage of the spectator from film to film (and from stream to stream in the programme) is not merely given free rein but also *mobilised* in a specific intellectual direction. 'There is a certain exhilaration to be derived from the glut of a festival diet, an excitement in the air and an energy which can be harnessed to make some intervention, to politicise the cultural.'[8]

The tension in Stern's piece between a fondness for the unprogrammable freedom of the spectator and, all the same, the desire to nudge that spectator in *some* way, to some extent, is palpable – and it is eloquent of the different directions in which contemporary festivals, then as now, inexorably pull. (Of the Australian festivals, it is Brisbane that does the best, most progressive job of steering a path between these conflicting tendencies of the 'free marketplace' and the 'cultural experience'.) Stern wisely sees in the pedagogic, community-forming dream of the festival-watching cinephile – which usually expresses itself in a frustrated critique of the festivals we have as hotbeds of compromise and mediocrity – a certain kind of overdetermination or over-investment, arising precisely from the 'here and elsewhere' mentality so constitutive of social life in Australia:

> Much of this railing seems to me to be indicative of the poverty of film culture in Australia, and the isolation experienced here, the sense of exclusion from overseas developments. The festival assumes undue importance as a target, we demand that it be, not all things to all people, but that it should be the acme of a radical film culture, representing all that is lacking elsewhere – i.e., it should be challenging of the status quo, uncompromisingly committed to alternative film practices, dedi-

cated to the cultivation of political and theoretical issues, and disengaged from marketing practices.[9]

The reading, by an Australian cinephile in 2008, of this entirely reasonable account has, however, a grimly ironic pay-off: Stern ends her train of thought here by suggesting that 'such demands should be addressed, and more appropriately, to bodies such as the Australian Film Institute'[10] – a relentlessly mainstream organisation that has, in recent years, rather like the British Film Institute, systematically divested itself of most of its cultural functions (maintaining a library, distributing and exhibiting independent local films, enabling publications and seminars) in order to identify itself more closely with 'the industry'. More than ever, film festivals can come to seem like Utopias arriving from the Great Elsewhere, like the three-ring circus come to a small town…

Has the audience – any audience – slipped through the cracks of all these momentous, paradoxical, contradictory changes in the nature of festivals? There is, indeed, one further, still more insidious cultural turn to record. What we have witnessed, in the larger circuit of international film culture, is a new sort of disconnection or dissociation: between the arthouse chains and the festivals. For a long time, the two existed in symbiosis, and even moved in lockstep: arthouse distributors would preview their latest acquisitions at a high-profile festival screening (such as Opening or Closing Night), and then go on to shop around for new product among the programme offerings. This relationship often indeed became rather too close for comfort, with certain festivals coming to increasingly resemble vast, compliant 'showcases' for upcoming arthouse product. Today, however, there is a growing, yawning autonomy between these two realms of arthouse and festival – summed up in the recent creation of a truly hideous term: the 'festival film', which is apparently the name for a film whose destiny, nowadays, is *only* to play (on the big screen, at least) on the international festival circuit.

What this means, in practice, is that, in many countries, the films prized by progressive cinephiles – the films of Philippe Garrel, Pedro Costa, Apichatpong Weerasethakul, and many others – are branded, virtually from the outset of their public life, as unfit for general (or even moderately specialised) distribution and exhibition. Another delicious anecdote marks, for me, the beginning of this historic transformation: the tale of certain arthouse buyers who had skipped (as 'not their kind of thing') the screening of the Dardennes' *Rosetta* at Cannes in 1999, and were then shocked when the main jury (headed by Cronenberg) gave it two major prizes. This kind of wilful blindness to vast portions of world cinema – and many modes of filmmaking – is increasingly evident everywhere.

In this rather ominous context, the festival audience – cinephile or otherwise – may yet again find itself transformed into a community that is 'all in this together', huddled around those ephemeral, magical 'festival films' that manage to squeeze themselves through our narrowing cultural portals.

Notes

1   Bruce Hodsdon (2007) 'Notes From the Edge: The 16th Brisbane International Film Festival', *Senses of Cinema*, 45 (October–December). Available at: < http:// www.sensesofcinema.com/contents/festivals/07/45/brisbane-iff-2007.html> accessed: 23 August, 2008.

2   Ibid.

3   Staying with Australian writings that may not be well-known elsewhere, I also recommend two remarkable collective pieces of creative/experimental writing about the poetics and politics of the festival-going experience, both of which appeared in the leftist journal *Arena* in the guise of reviews of the Melbourne Film Festival: Fiona Mackie, Scott McQuire and Nikos Papastergiades (1986) 'The Technological Dream Factory', *Arena*, 76, 97–115; and 'Sphinx L'Amour' (1987) 'Kaleidoscope: A Festival of Films', *Arena*, 80, 49–63.

4   Kathe Boehringer and Stephen Crofts (1980) 'The Triumph of Taste', *The Australian Journal of Screen Theory*, 8, 69–79.

5   Ibid.: 75.

6   See John Hinde (1981) *Other People's Pictures*. Sydney: ABC Books.

7   Lesley Stern (1981) 'The Melbourne Film Festival', *Filmnews* (September), 6–7, 13.

8   Ibid.: 7.

9   Ibid.: 6.

10   Ibid.: 7.

III.

MEMOIRS AND CASE STUDIES

Asian Film Festivals and Their Diminishing Glitter Domes: An Appraisal of PIFF, SIFF and HKIFF

STEPHEN TEO

The establishment of film festivals in Asia as a form of cultural practice and recognition of cinema as an artistic medium was a process that began in the mid-1970s. Hong Kong provided a model that set the process in motion. The British colony (as it was then) was known as a manufacturing centre with a popular film industry, but its film culture was at best rudimentary, being spawned by local film buffs who could only watch limited selections of art films through organised film societies. By the late 1970s, Hong Kong was on its way to becoming a newly-industrialised economy. As its citizens became more educated and more affluent, calls were sounded to install a film festival devoted not to the commercial interests of the industry but to cinema as film culture and art. Such a type of film festival virtually did not exist in Asia – until the installation of the Hong Kong International Film Festival.[1]

The first edition of HKIFF, which took place in 1977, was devised as a festival organised by cinephiles for cinephiles. The festival was purely a showcase of films from all over the world, and there was no competition category. It soon gained a reputation over the years as a platform for Asian films.

The Hong Kong New Wave had gotten under way in 1979, and Asian films with hardly any international exposure at the time (films of the Philippines, Indonesia, Thailand, South Korea, Sri Lanka and so on) found a natural home at HKIFF. In fact, HKIFF became the most prestigious film festival in Asia in the 1980s for its comprehensive selections of the best of Asian cinemas. Hong Kong became known as the best festival for foreign critics to watch new Asian films and make discoveries which could then be introduced to the whole world. One of its most memorable moments occurred in 1985 when it premiered *The Yellow Earth* and presented the Fifth Generation filmmakers Chen Kaige and Zhang Yimou to audiences outside of China for the first time. Of equal importance to the esteem of HKIFF was the retrospective programmes of classic Hong Kong cinema, a permanent feature of the festival for some twenty-odd years until it was superceded by the Hong Kong Film Archive's own programming imperatives in 2001 (HKFA having been established the previous year).[2] HKIFF also ran retrospectives of Asian masters: Ozu, Gosho, Oshima, Naruse, Teguh Karya, Gerardo De Leon, Fei Mu, Zhu Shilin, Ritwik Ghatak, and Lester James Peries.

In the first ten or fifteen years of HKIFF, its importance as a seminal event in the film-cultural milieu of Hong Kong cannot be denied. It was a forum for Hong Kong and other Asian filmmakers to introduce their works to the watching world. In this regard, never was Hong Kong's role as a crossroads between East and West more pronounced than at HKIFF. The festival promoted the Hong Kong New Wave, the Fifth Generation, the Sixth Generation and the New Taiwan Cinema to the West, and it introduced the best of European cinemas to the East. The role of the festival was also to fasten the bonds between the Chinese filmmakers from Hong Kong, Taiwan and China and between them and an appreciative audience in Hong Kong – an important process in the growth of an 'alternative' artistic and more innovative strand of filmmaking in a community traditionally attuned to making money or making ends meet. It fostered a film culture where a local audience who could appreciate films was a morale booster for filmmakers who are otherwise constantly pressured into making commercial entertainments. HKIFF also provided the impetus for the rise of a more institutionalised film criticism through its publication of catalogues which are in fact more like critical journals, in particular, the bilingual catalogues devoted to the Hong

Kong Retrospective containing scholarly essays and valuable biographical and filmographical data. The retrospective paved the way for the establishment of a film archive committed to preserving and restoring old films of the Hong Kong cinema which normally ended up in trash bins.

On a personal level, HKIFF has meant a lot to my career as a critic and now as an academic, having been involved in the festival for over ten years from the mid-1980s onwards. I worked for HKIFF as the English editor and occasional translator of the Hong Kong retrospective catalogues. These retrospectives reintroduced to my memory the Cantonese and Mandarin films which I had watched in my childhood and teenage years as I grew up in the 1960s in a small town in Sarawak, Malaysia, where I was born. Watching these old films year after year for a period of about ten years was a reformative process. The retrospective programmes instilled in me a sense of self-awareness about my past and about my love for the cinema, prompting me towards a greater critical reassessment of films that were supposedly disposable as you watched them over the years but which were, in the Freudian sense of the term, screen memories forever embedded in my unconsciousness that could be reawakened at any time of one's adult life and reinvigorate the ego.

In real life, the effect of these screen memories was to reorient my cinematic direction and worldview. I became fixated on re-evaluating the relevance and significance of old Cantonese films, which were commonly termed by the Hong Kong public *tsaan pin* – meaning damaged or deficient films. Along with the notions of historical, sociological and anthropological value in reassessing the old Hong Kong cinema, I began to reappraise them in terms of their *cinematic value*. This was the theoretical gist of the change in my critical direction, which came as a sort of epiphany in that I realised I had wiped out a part of my memory (the old Hong Kong cinema) in my development as a critic. Just as HKIFF found an identity through its focus on Asian cinemas, I too found an identity through the images of the new generations of directors in Hong Kong, China, Taiwan and other East Asian and Southeast Asian countries. Names like King Hu, Hou Hsiao-hsien, Edward Yang, Ann Hui, Tsui Hark, Johnnie To, Wong Kar-wai, Tsai Ming-liang, Tian Zhuangzhuang, Jia Zhangke, Kim Ki-duk, Apichatpong Weerasethakul, and many others, have imprinted themselves into my mind and have certainly fostered and sustained my identity as an Asian critic and writer. Hence, the festival was a source of personal growth as well as an indispensable venue for the enjoyment of films from all over the world, but particularly from Asia. For me, it was a base of handy research into the Hong Kong cinema (both the old Hong Kong cinema and the cinemas of the New Wave and Second Wave), which prepared the groundwork for the writing of my first book, *Hong Kong Cinema: The Extra Dimensions*, published by the British Film Institute in 1997.

HKIFF was also an inspiration for other film festivals in Asia, primarily the Singapore International Film Festival (SIFF) and South Korea's Pusan International Film Festival (PIFF), setting the standards for these festivals to adopt and build upon. Both Singapore and South Korea share with Hong Kong similar developmental histories from manufacturing into newly-industrialised status. Both countries have strong film cultures, with South Korea possessing a film industry that became highly competitive from the mid-1990s onwards. Singapore, with no film industry to speak of for most of the 1970s and 1980s, began to develop its own industry in the 1990s. SIFF (its first edition in 1987) and PIFF, established in 1996, both imitated the 'Asian showcase' model of HKIFF as well as the principle of promoting one's own domestic films and independent filmmakers. SIFF, when it came along, was a timely forum for a group of young filmmakers who made short films and later went on to make features, bringing international recognition to Singapore and driving the impulses in governing circles to support the creation of a local film industry. Similarly, PIFF has been a constructive platform for South Korean directors of all shades to exhibit their wares. At the same time, both festivals have primed their objectives toward promoting Asian cinemas, with PIFF being the most ambitious of the three festivals. All three share not only the same objectives but also largely the same programming structures; all look fairly alike such that they may be triplets born of the same love of film, which is not to imply that there is any strong brotherly love between the three.

In point of fact, all three festivals are rivals to a certain extent. SIFF and PIFF have tried to displace Hong Kong as the most attractive, most prestigious venue for Asian cinemas. PIFF, with its institutional and governmental support, is by far the most successful in this endeavour. SIFF, with its shrink-

South Korea's Pusan International Film Festival has quickly become one of the most important film events in Asia

ing audience base and cutbacks in government funding, has floundered after successful runs in the 1990s as the Southeast Asian hub of Asian films, but has continued to emphasise its focus on Southeast Asian films. Meanwhile, the original model, HKIFF, has unfortunately become a model of another kind in the era following Hong Kong's handover to China in 1997 – the sort of model where film festivals try bravely to maintain their reputations against fierce competition from other film festivals in the region and from shifting trends and habits in cinema viewing and film culture which are cutting into the effectiveness of film festivals and their reason for being.

In the immediate post-1997 era, HKIFF had sought to break away from the government and become an independent-run festival. Independence was a catch-cry in the countdown period to the 1997 handover. The Chinese government had come up with a policy in the early 1990s to pressurise film festivals around the world to cancel controversial films banned on the mainland, failing which they would withdraw officially-approved films selected for the festival. The crunch point came in 1994 when China's Film Industry Administration (FIA) protested HKIFF's selection of banned films, including Tian Zhuangzhuang's *The Blue Kite* and Zhang Yuan's *Beijing Bastards*, by withdrawing nine films from the festival, sparking off a robust debate in the Hong Kong press over the Mainland's censorship policy and its tactic of withdrawing films.[3] The resulting standoff between programming staff who naturally insisted on the right of programming independence and Chinese film officials who insisted on their right to censor became something of a deadly exercise over the remaining years of the 1990s. The Hong Kong Government found itself embarrassingly caught in the middle. Thus, when the momentum for HKIFF to become independent became stronger in the post-1997 years, the Government, always keen to placate China, was more than willing to let go of the film festival.

Since 2004, HKIFF has been fully 'privatised', as the jargon at the time put it. It exists now as a 'non-profit, non-government organisation', running year-round programmes on top of the film festival proper held annually over the Easter holiday period. One major change to the festival is that it now stages several competition events as a tactic to stay competitive with Pusan. To some critics, this has changed the nature of HKIFF in that it is no longer a purely cinephilic festival but one where competitions have become a routine part of its organisation. The competition events, entailing cash prizes and the need to invite international jurors, have raised the financial burden on the festival. As a non-profit society, HKIFF must depend on commercial sponsors to shore up its operating budget, supplemented by aid from government-funded agencies such as the Hong Kong Arts Development Council. The post-1997 years have, however, not been good financially for Hong Kong with the territory falling into a state of recession due to the slump in property prices which occurred well before the handover. But almost from the start of the handover, Hong Kong had experienced a run of crises, from the Asian financial meltdown (which precipitated a crash in the Hong Kong stock market in October 1997) to the outbreak of bird flu to the outbreak of SARS – all of which produced economic consequences (a fall in tourism, contracting retail sales, deteriorating trade and unemployment) which have contributed to the overall sense of doom in Hong Kong (famously portrayed in the *Infernal Affairs* trilogy) from which it is only now slowly recovering.

In addition, the Hong Kong film industry itself has gone further into the doldrums since 1997, a decline exacerbated by the increasing dominance of Hollywood blockbusters at the local box-office and the rise of other Asian competitors, notably the South Korean film industry, which have encroached on Hong Kong's traditional markets in Southeast Asia. In fact, an unprecedented 'Korean wave' of films, TV drama, culinary culture, fashion and pop music, has swept through East Asia. Over this period, the Pusan International Film Festival has grown in status by becoming Asia's premier film festival. For most international critics, PIFF has replaced Hong Kong as the 'best place to watch Asian films', not to mention new Korean films. HKIFF's status has suffered in comparison, and one could ask whether it can recover its former glory if it was a question of going back to the past. The point here may be that it does not matter terribly that HKIFF is no longer the premier Asian festival or the 'best place to watch Asian films'. It is perhaps sufficient that HKIFF maintain itself and satisfy the first requirement of any festival – to bring and provide the best works of international film culture to its local citizens?

Like the Singapore International Film Festival, HKIFF is suffering from a lack of institutional and governmental support. A major institutional sponsor, the airline Cathay-Pacific, dropped out of supporting the festival in 2004. But unlike SIFF, HKIFF appears to be doing a better job in staging glitzy events which have the effect of concealing any sense of crisis or financial hardship from the public. It also managed not to cut back on its programmes, such that the 31st edition in 2007, held from 20 March to 11 April is the longest run in HKIFF history, and indeed, the longest run of any festival anywhere. As if that wasn't enough, it also began a month-long 'Summer IFF' from July to August. All this suggests that HKIFF is putting on a brave, confident face to demonstrate that the festival continues to have strong support from the public and from international critics, though this image has been dented somewhat with the revelation of the director Peter Tsi's resignation in September 2008 and the report that his departure had followed 'a period of mounting tension' within the organisation, because Tsi 'had long been outspoken on the need for more financial and promotional support for the festival from government sources'.[4]

The Hong Kong Government, keen to support the film industry if not so much the film festival, has continued to show at least spiritual support for

HKIFF by staging its Hong Kong International Film and Television Market (Filmart), organised by the government's Trade and Development Council, around the festival period.[5] In addition to Filmart, there are co-presentations of the Hong Kong-Asia Film Financing Forum (HAF)[6] and the Hong Kong Film Awards (the 'Hong Kong Oscars') presentation ceremony. The pomp and glitter of all these events no doubt camouflage any sense of crisis or desperation. In contrast with HKIFF, SIFF's 20th-anniversary edition in 2007 was a much-reduced festival, a sad shadow of itself in its halcyon days in the mid-1990s when the Singapore Government was fully committed not only to supporting art and culture but a burgeoning film industry. Perhaps SIFF could draw a lesson from HKIFF, which is that in order to maintain a façade of normalcy amidst uncertain times, it needs to stage its own array of glittering events, all sponsored and government-funded (suggestions of a Southeast Asia Film Fund and a Southeast Asia film market, for example, have been mooted). In this way, it might surmount its current crisis and go on to better things. This is of course easier said than done, and it may well be that the time for SIFF to stage pomp and glitter has passed and it needs now to concentrate on the substance of its programmes and revivify itself this way.

Yet while both SIFF and HKIFF may be caught in a funding pitfall, they need at the same time to justify themselves in times of shifting paradigms in the watching and the experiencing of films. Younger generations of audiences are growing up with instant programmes available through different media and sources (YouTube, downloadable films, DVDs, and so forth). The medium and apparatus of film are undergoing a digital metamorphosis. The downside of this is the tendency for shorter attention spans and the lack of contexts, with little or no perspectives of history. Alongside these seismic shifts, there are internal questions over festival management and direction that need to be addressed for both SIFF and HKIFF, with lessons perhaps to be heeded by PIFF and other newcomer Asian festivals, such as that of Bangkok and Shanghai.

The concern here is that of change and renewal as the idea of cinema itself is changing before our eyes. In many ways, this might threaten the continuing viability of film festivals such as the three in focus, which all came into existence through a love of film culture in its traditional form. For Hong Kong, the stakes may be higher in that the film festival's future is essentially tied up with larger concerns over Hong Kong's integration with China and the long-term survival of the domestic film industry. Against such a background, the thought that the film festival might not survive seems unwarranted. However, as in the case of SIFF, there is real concern over whether the festival can be attractive and relevant to newer, younger audiences and their environment of new digital technology and inter-digital media (IDM). At the same time, how does a festival keep its old guard happy by emphasising the need to show films in their classic celluloid form as well as the necessity to revive old films even if restored and possibly refashioned into digital form? How does it then educate the young to appreciate older films? The Generations X and Y almost certainly would not experience the same kind of epiphany as I did in watching older Asian films. What would be their film-watching epiphany, as they look back, say, on the films of the Hong Kong New Wave, the Fifth Generation and the New Taiwan Cinema (films made either before they were born or were just children)?

Such questions have arisen in part because the management, including directors and programmers, that runs both SIFF and HKIFF have been in place for a long time. The same people who ran SIFF at its inception twenty years ago are still running it today – a sign that the organisation is sorely in need of generational change. Similarly, certain key programming personnel in HKIFF have been in place for many years. The continuity provided by this permanent staff presence is perhaps all for the good, but it could also be another source of anxiety as times change and newer blood is called for. A group of permanently-installed programmers might inspire nothing more than rigidity and a business-as-usual mentality when the business itself is undergoing change and paradigms are shifting. The objective of promoting Asian cinemas, for example, is not an unchanging aim.

There are as many different Asian cinemas as there are many Asian film festivals which have adopted 'Asian cinema' as their flagship (in fact, all Asian film festivals worth their salt cannot but proclaim the promotion of Asian cinema as their mission). Apart from SIFF, PIFF and HKIFF, there are other smaller festivals in Asia championing the Asian film cause, not to mention festivals in Europe and elsewhere. New trends and the rise of new Asian cinemas need new visions, which probably entail a new generation of programmers. SIFF has become an urgent case model for new direction and generational change in that its focus on Asian films tends to appear tired and stale. While the films themselves might have reflected genuinely new trends and exciting new work, their promotion is often lacklustre as if the programmers themselves don't quite believe that the public will buy a hard sell. At HKIFF, selling new Asian films from relatively unknown cinemas (such as the new Malaysian cinema, for example) to a notoriously chauvinistic public where Asian films are concerned is always a tough call and the programming of these films tends to look *de rigueur*.

It goes without saying that Asian film festivals need a new vision of Asian cinema. People who have been in the business of programming Asian films for a long time may just take the vision thing for granted, assuming that their subjective tastes and views will always be that of the public they serve. HKIFF and SIFF are both caught in this quagmire, carrying on year after year without articulating anything amounting to a vision and taking for granted that the public knows what their vision of Asian cinema is. Only PIFF has come up with something close to a vision, for example in pushing the idea of 'Pan-Asian' cooperation and film funding in its successful implementation of the 'Pusan Promotion Plan' (PPP), which HKIFF has tried to imitate with HAF, and the Asian Film Market (launched in 2006) which will take over the PPP and expand into newer areas of the Asian continent and beyond. A new initiative, the 'Asian Cinema Fund' (ACF), has zeroed in on the aim to 'promote Asian cinema and discover new talents in young Asian filmmakers'.[7] In this way, PIFF has succeeded in becoming a region-wide forum where HKIFF and SIFF have failed, but it is far from clear that it has secured a victory in the vision battle over hearts and minds of Asian cinephiles. Its success with PPP, instituted in 1998, one year after the Asian financial crisis, is merely a reflection of the strength and determination of institutional and governmental support and funding. PIFF is not infallible, and over time if it hasn't already, it might falter due to the same problems of paradigm shift, generational change and internal renewal.

PIFF is the youngest of the three festivals and if we go by the truism of Asian families that the youngest son is always treated better than the oldest and the middle sons, time and circumstance have been kinder to PIFF. It has learned from the experiences of HKIFF and SIFF and its leadership has the political will and means to back up the objectives of the festival for as long as needed. PIFF is therefore on a roll insofar as its Asian vision is guaranteed thus far by government support, helped along by the immense goodwill generated by the soft power of the 'Korean wave' sweeping through the region. But soft power by virtue of its nature is highly malleable and unpredictable. There could be a backlash, and a rollback of the Korean wave is not out of the question in the foreseeable future. PIFF has to prepare for such a contingency, but for the moment it is safe to say that just in staying the course, it is way ahead of HKIFF and SIFF.

PIFF's success so far is also due to its utilisation of foreign critics, primarily European critics, to promote itself and the South Korean cinema in international circles by word of mouth and through publications. Both HKIFF and SIFF have in the past relied on these same foreign critics to sell their festivals and cinemas, but since the status of HKIFF and SIFF have each fallen relative to that of PIFF, the role of the foreign critics must be viewed skeptically. Clearly, such critics have their own self-interest in mind, but on the positive side, it must be acknowledged that there are many foreign critics who are genuine scholars drawn to Asian film festivals by the love of film, driven by the desire to learn and understand, and engage in real and constructive dialogues with Asian filmmakers and critics, giving sustenance to the concept of exchange and communication between Asia and the rest of the world. In the final analysis, how film festivals can function on this level of cinephilia and pedagogy is the key question. Too often, film festivals end up like markets where one is forced to haggle over goods and prices and to avoid powerful transnational interests seeking to control and dominate sections of the market if not the whole thing.

Because all the three major Asian film festivals analysed in this article are basically similar, their fates and fortunes appear intertwined. They are similar in that they are the three most important festivals in Asia because of their locations – all strategic hubs on the East Asian mainland stretching from the northeast to southeast – and because of their stated aim of promoting Asian cinema. They mirror each other in terms of failure and success. They are not equal, to be sure, but they tread the same path, and if it can be said that one is in decline, the others might follow. The thesis of this article is that all three festivals have the same concerns about failure because of structural reasons while the success of one cannot be repeated on the same level by the others.

In other words, success can never be equitably distributed which means that each must diverge from the path they follow, by finding their own road to success. In this way, success can only be defined by how each festival from now on surmounts its crises and anxieties and faces the challenges ahead.

But perhaps the festivals will just go on regardless. The glitter dome of the cinema will continue to shine and sparkle irrespective of shifting paradigms and changing apparatus. No evidence exists to suggest that cinema is dying or even that it is in terminal old age. The cinema has survived the coming of sound, colour, TV and video, and it will survive the entry of new digital media into its glittering dome – in effect to add to the glitter. Film festivals are only as good as the films, and on this principle, Asian film festivals have even more reason to continue indefinitely because Asian cinemas will become more not less dynamic and newer cinemas and generations will rise. The sense that HKIFF and SIFF are drifting downwards may be only temporary, due to the conditions of the film industries (one in decline while the other is just small). When conditions change for the better, the festivals may rediscover their sense of purpose. Film festivals have the capacity to never fade away even as the glitter domes diminish, which is after all why every major city in Asia wants its own film festival – and smaller cities too get in on the act.

Notes

1   In the 1950s film industries in the region created the 'Asian Film Festival', launched in 1954 and overseen by a federation of motion picture producers. The festival travelled from country to country as an industry-sponsored competitive event, emphasising the glamour of movies and showcasing the best-produced films by the major film studios in the region. Hong Kong's Shaw Brothers Studio was a major player in the Asian Film Festival in the 1950s and 1960s. See the link to the Asian Film Festival page at the Shaw Brothers website http://shaw.sg/sw_about.aspx. Accessed: 24 August, 2008. Cindy Hing-yuk Wong has described the Asian Film Festival as 'primarily a public relations event for the industries' which is a fair description of the event, and as such, the Asian Film Festival cannot be considered a film festival in the modern sense of the term indicating a festival presenting hundreds of films

from all over the world, independently chosen and free from the influence of the studios, film companies and their vested interests. See Cindy Hing-yuk Wong (2007) 'Distant screens: Film festivals and the global projection of Hong Kong cinema', in Gina Marchetti and Tan See-kam (eds) *Hong Kong Film, Hollywood and the New Global Cinema: No Film is an Island*. London and New York: Routledge, 177–92. The Asian Film Festival was reconstituted in 1982 as the 'Asia-Pacific Film Festival', which continues to run to the present day without attracting much attention. I was a member of the jury, which also included Jonathan Rosenbaum, in the 1991 Asia-Pacific Film Festival held in Taipei, and we awarded the Best Picture prize to Edward Yang's *A Brighter Summer Day*.

2   Although the HKFA has taken over the programming of the retrospective programme, it continues to be associated with the HKIFF in that the programme is always scheduled to take place during the run of the HKIFF and it is printed in the Festival's programme brochure, but it is separately administered and the films are shown in the HKFA's own theatre venue, so technically, it is not a part of HKIFF. The HKFA has year-round programmes of its own.

3   See Chan Wai-fong and Daniel Kwan (1994), 'Censors' shadow cast over screens', *South China Morning Post*, 21 March, 17. The Chinese side put their case in Hong Kong's Chinese press, arguing that HKIFF had 'agreed' to their request for not showing banned films. See 'Beijing zuo fuhan benbao, zhi gangfang ceng zuo chengnuo' ('Beijing's reply, Hong Kong had agreed'), *Xinbao (Hong Kong Economic Journal)*, 19 March 2004, 23.

4   See Patrick Frater, 'Tsi quits as HK festival director', http://www.varietyasiaonline. com/content/view/2044/. Accessed: 24 August, 2008.

5   See 'The Unprecedented United Front by Filmart, HAF, & HKIFF 2007', http://gbcode.tdctrade.com/gb/www.tdctrade.com/dm/cp339728/index.htm. Accessed; 24 August, 2008.

6   HAF was first launched in 2000 as a film industry initiative. It was then discontinued only to be reinstituted in 2003 but was cancelled due to the outbreak of SARS. It became operative again the following year. For more on the original HAF, see the HKIFF booklet *The Age of Independents: New Asian Film and Video*, published by the 24th HKIFF, 2000, 42–3. See also Lily Kong (2005), 'The Sociality of Cultural Industries: Hong Kong's Cultural Policy and Film Industry', *International Journal of Cultural Policy*, 11, 1, 61–76.

7   Quoted from the FIPRESCI Circular 4/2007 (July 19 2007), 1.

The Sad Case of the Bangkok Film Festival

KONG RITHDEE

To recount the brief history of the Bangkok International Film Festival (BKKIFF) involves plunging the reader into swamps of rumours, scorn, management scuffles, confusing shifts of power and incidents of shameful corruption. Please don't wince – the history of the festival included good news and good-hearted people, and originally I would have loved to open the article on a more optimistic note with the story of those who struggled and clung to their faith to initiate the idea of a movie festival in a country, like Thailand, that barely grasps the concept of cinema as an art form. But unfortunately, a vile scandal broke out in December 2007 while this anthology was starting to take shape, and it turned out to be a scandal that not only brought shame to the BKKIFF and the Thai people, but probably constitutes one of the most shocking infamies in the history of international film festivals. It also serves as a cautionary tale on how a film festival could be exploited by crafty bureaucrats and businessmen, at the expense of cinephiles and taxpayers' money.

It was then that the US Department of Justice announced that it had arrested an American couple, Gerald Green and his wife Patricia, for bribing the governor of the Tourism Authority of Thailand (TAT). TAT has been the sponsor of BKKIFF since 2002, and the $1.7-million kickbacks were paid, according to the FBI report, so that Mr Green's company, the L.A.-based Film Festival Management Inc., could be awarded the contract to organise the festival between 2003 and 2006. This scandalous report, like all

Poster for the 2008 edition of the problem-ridden Bangkok International Film Festival

kinds of embarrassing news, spread through the world's filmmaking community in a matter of hours. In Bangkok, we sighed: just when you thought the reputation of the BKKIFF couldn't get any worse, it did.

The FBI affidavit didn't directly name the Thai official who allegedly took the bribe. The TAT governor during that period was Juthamas Siriwan, who promptly held a press conference denying any involvement. A day later however, Ms. Juthamas resigned from the political party she belonged to and pulled out of Thailand's general election three days before voters went to the polls. At the time of going to print, the Thai anti-graft agency are still working in co-operation with the FBI to prove the crime, or the innocence, of those likely to be involved in the fraud. Yet as most Thais know, hardly any high-ranking Thai officials are ever convicted of high-profile corruption crimes, and we keep our fingers crossed that justice will be honoured this time around.

Without any intention to rub salt on the wound, I'm recounting the incident fully aware that the bribery scandal was a final humiliation to this troubled festival of my home city, and that it represents a perfect opportunity for the government to rethink the management and funding of this notoriously expensive event. After BKKIFF's 2007 edition, having been moved to July from January, there was uncertainty whether TAT would continue to host the festival – or whether the festival would continue to exist at all. Then in December 2007, it looked likely that BKKIFF would go on despite the bloody *coup de grace* brought on courtesy of Mr Green and the FBI. In September 2008, the festival finally took place with the Federation of National Film Association of Thailand as the organiser, while TAT, still the sponsor, lowered its involvement. But then again the fate of BKKIFF 2009 remains unclear largely due to the current economic crisis. One thing is dead certain though: the L.A.-based firm, reportedly with little experience in managing a film festival even though it's called Film Festival Management Inc, would not re-emerge to get any contract from the still-shocked-and-awed TAT.

Still, with grudging optimism, we can regard this scam as a cleansing agent that can help to purge old demons and encourage a new chapter of BKKIFF. So perhaps it helps to go back to review the birth of movie festivals in Thailand in the mid-1990s, and to gauge the degree of local cinephilia and government support that are always the blood vessels of most major cinefests. In the global climate when film festivals have become everything from political tools to tourism magnets – sometimes even to celebrate good films – the tale from Bangkok is a worthy case study.

The early years

Though Thai films enjoyed halcyon days in the 1960s when as many as 200 titles were produced each year, the historical mindset was that cinema was strictly a form of lowly entertainment. The idea of the movies as an arm of cultural identity and academic curiosity was thin on the ground. Likewise, in terms of economic spur: while Hong Kong pioneered its festival in the late 1970s during the peak of its homegrown moviemaking business, the concept of 'selling' Thai cinema to overseas audiences didn't gain ground until only lately. And while foreign critics had good reasons to fly to the former British colony to check out new Asian harvests in the 1980s, hardly anybody outside Thailand took Siamese films seriously until Pen-ek Ratanaruang, Nonzee Nimibutr, Wisit Sasanatieng and Apichatpong Weerasethakul burst onto the scene in the late 1990s.

In those years before film festivals, Bangkok cinephiles haunted various institutions to consume non-American titles. The Alliance Francaise, the Goethe Institute, the British Council and the Japan Foundation organised regular screenings in their auditoriums (as they still do now), and those places saw the gatherings of small legions of film students and enthusiasts craving for alternatives from Hollywood dominance. If nothing else, this testifies that even though the potent stimuli that would engender a film festival was absent, the interest in filmgoing as a cultural practice has always been here, albeit marginalised.

The first time the term 'film festival' was officially used in Thailand was in 1995, when American expatriate Scott Rosenberg, together with the Thai National Film Archive and film historian Dome Sukhawong, organised the BOI Film Festival. Even though the venue and surroundings were a little unusual, it was a small, well-intentioned event. The festival was funded by the Thai Board of Investment (BOI), and it took place as part of the BOI Fair, a vast exhibition of Thai machinery and investment opportunities on a dusty ground fair near an industrial port in the eastern province of Chonburi. Thai films were shown along with selections from Southeast Asia. Despite being a trailblazer in a way, it's unclear how much the BOI Film Festival actually influenced the subsequent attempts to put together local cine-affairs in later years.

Before we move on to the birth of BKKIFF, it must be noted that, in 1997, a significant but often overlooked movie event was started in Bangkok. Modest, friendly and always struggling, the Thai Short Film and Video Festival was originated by the Thai Film Foundation, led by Chalida Uabumrungjit, and until today it still best represents the spirit of a film festival as an event where the joy of making movies is celebrated among like-minded people. Its limited funding usually comes from different cultural agencies, but the festival has over the years matured into a crucial gathering of film students and independent filmmakers. The festival threw its 11th edition in August 2007, and it is now the longest-running film festival in Thailand.

With the emphasis on local shorts, the Thai Short Film and Video Festival has been programming shorts from other countries, especially from Asia, since its first year. To put forward a bold supposition, it's fair to say that this is the festival that has been following the right direction (perhaps unintentionally) from the get-go – that is, to establish Bangkok as a cultural hub for moving images in the region of Southeast Asia.

Perhaps spurred by the growth of Asian films in the global market and by the enthusiasm for 'New Thai Cinema', the first Bangkok Film Festival (BFF, note the absence of 'International') was founded in September 1998. Two forces made it possible: *The Nation* newspaper sponsored the event and another American in Bangkok, former IBM staff member and movie enthusiast Brian Bennett, became the programmer. Without the fanfare and pseudo-glitz that would later became the mark of the festival's later reincarnations, the first BFF took place at the multiplex on the sixth floor of the Emporium, a stylish department store on Sukhumvit Road. The programming included American independent cinema, which Bennett favoured, and a fair share of Asian titles.

That first edition was borne by the air of cultural curiosity, perhaps a headlong naiveté – even the sponsor plunged into the project without a clear idea of what it would yield. And despite the quibble that it ignored the local film industry, the first BFF was a success. To a certain extent, it became the outlet of local cinephilia as well as a widely publicised event that attracted the attention of regular multiplex-goers. It introduced the idea of alternative cinema to general audiences, especially young people who had been spoon-fed by Hollywood staples, and a number of them seemed to catch the bug.

In a less cheerful light, the 1998 festival also featured a controversial run-in with the censors – that unshakable demon whose path is inseparable from the development of Siamese movie culture – when the police raided the festival office and banned two films, the Singaporean *Bugis Street*, because of its nudity, and the Thai experimental short *My Teacher Eats Biscuits*, directed by Ing K and Brian Bennett himself, for its unsavoury portrayal of monks. (It would take a whole article to discuss the Thai censorship law, a model of supreme frustration usually enforced by arbitrary judgement of the powers-that-be. In 2007, for example, BKKIFF screened the orgy-strewn *Shortbus* without anyone batting an eyelid. In December 2007, the new Film Act was passed by Parliament to replace the Jurassic one used since 1930, and although it finally initiated the rating system, it retains the right of the State to cut or ban films.)

For most critics, the Siamese New Wave began with the release of Nonzee Nimibutr's *Daeng Bireley and Young Gangsters* in 1997, the year that Thailand suffered a shocking economic meltdown. One year later, BFF was founded. It's worth observing the inverse fates of the movies and the country's economic health. Was the film industry Teflon-coated? (No.) Was the economy's morass actually not that dire as people assumed? (No.) Was it true that people turn to movies for distraction because times were tough? (No, but maybe yes, or perhaps no.) Was the creative juice of filmmakers flowing because of social depression? (Ideally, yes.) Was it the force of globalisation that ripened our cultural hunger in films? (Again, perhaps yes, but maybe no). How come we had the willingness and the wherewithal to spend money on something inherently trivial and expensive like making movies, and organising a movie festival? This was probably a manifestation of the crazy logic that sometimes influences Thai reality.

In any case, *The Nation* and Bennett ran the BFF for three years – until the American was relieved of his duties after the 2000 edition. In 2001, *The Nation* hired independent filmmaker/lecturer Pimpaka Towira to programme the festival, which by that time had grown into a solid annual event devotedly followed by the expanding ranks of Bangkok cinephiles. Foreign guests had started to arrive, too, partly because of the budding reputation of the Thai New Wave. But then a new twist came, along with another set of Americans.

The later years

People wonder why BKKIFF doesn't specify its age in the banner (say, the 34th HKIFF, or the 60th Festival de Cannes; instead we have BKKIFF 2006 or 2007). That's because the confusion over the paradigm shift that occurred after its 2001 edition made the count impossible, or at least problematic.

When Pimpaka left the fourth BFF to make her feature film, *The Nation* hired Kriangsak 'Victor' Silakong to chair the BFF. The former actor/play director set about picking films and completed his programming in mid-2002, a few months before the scheduled event in September. That was when the Tourism Authority of Thailand stepped in. Foreseeing the potential of the cinefest as one of the flagship spectacles in its annual tourism calendar, the TAT 'took over' the festival, while the original host, *The Nation*, was contracted to be the organiser. Although Kriangsak had wrapped his selection and the festival was ready to roll, TAT demanded that the festival be pushed from September 2002 to January 2003, because, as my source confirms, that was the only month in the year that TAT had no other events. Squeezed tightly between Rotterdam and Gothenberg and Berlin, the 'new' festival was launched with the title Bangkok International Film Festival 2003.

TAT duly promoted tourism as the main objective of BKKIFF. To achieve its desired level of glitz and glamour, the tourism people, who admitted on several occasions that they knew nothing about movies, hired the L.A.-based Film Festival Management Inc. (FFM), owned by Gerald Green, to organise special gala events and to fly in 'celebrities' (some of the biggest names that year include Steven Seagal; meanwhile Kriangsak got Agnès Varda to come and present a retrospective of her films). Inevitably, the cost ballooned from 20 million baht to 150 and eventually to 200 million baht (US$4–5 million). The venue was moved to downtown multiplexes around Siam Square and Rajaprasong.

Although moviegoers relished a larger inventory of films and the atmosphere of excitement whipped up by huge publicity, critics and industry people bemoaned the obvious lack of relevance; BKKIFF was designed to be a spectacle, photo-ops galore, and did not concern itself with fostering the film-going culture among locals. This quickly led to a conflict of creative interest, and *The Nation* decided to split from TAT after January 2003 to set up its own cinefest. Since it would be confusing go back to use the title BFF, Kriangsak came up with an entirely new name – World Film Festival of Bangkok. Small yet steady, the WFFBKK, which debuted in October 2003, hosted its sixth edition in 2008 and has over the years played a solid part in bringing in good films. Each year it costs the organiser around 20 million baht to put together the fest.

Back to BKKIFF: once *The Nation* departed, the TAT virtually handed over the festival to the Americans. FFM handled the programming (except the Southeast Asian section), inviting 'guests', flying in 'celebrities' and conjuring up all the red-carpet hullabaloo. Foreign journalists were flown in on business class, put up in luxurious hotels, and they were often shepherded not to the cinema but to sightseeing trips around Bangkok. Still, the screenings had no Thai subtitles, there were no discounts for students, at some Q&A sessions there were no Thai translators (this improved from 2006). In general, the festival curiously lacked the local touch; all it seemed to care about was the gala screenings and the glitz surrounding the movies rather than the movies themselves.

TAT issued a press release declaring that BKKIFF is 'one of the top ten film festivals in the world'. When it introduced the first Bangkok Film Market in 2006 at the Paragon Hall, it was a paltry, poorly-attended affair and by the second day most booths were deserted as exhibitors went to have foot massages. But, perplexingly, the press release painted a completely opposite picture by calling it a success. I understand that the ability to cocoon yourself in a totally different plain of reality, to shut out what the rest of the world is saying about you, is sometimes necessary. But not when you're throwing taxpayers' money around like there's no tomorrow.

In light of the recent bribery scandal, it could look as if I'm gleefully joining the winning team and arrogantly stomping on the chest of a fall guy by berating the 'Americanised' BKKIFF and the dubious decision of TAT to let FFM run the show at an expensive price tag. But all this criticism has been raised by critics and observers since 2004; in fact, I feel like repeating myself for the 99th time. In 2006, a Thai movie magazine printed a satirical cartoon in which a cinephile complains that he's reluctant to attend BKKIFF because it has been 'colonised'. It sounded a tad harsh, though frankly I'm tempted to agree. And now that the white people have left with the loot of Aztec gold, the 'natives' are left to clean up the mess.

But the problems are rooted deeper than the gaffe with the L.A. guys. It would be shortsighted to blame outsiders who simply exploited our gullibility and ignored our own shortcomings. A lot of people believed all our troubles would be solved when the new TAT governor cancelled the contract with FFM in late 2006 and asked Kriangsak and *The Nation* to temporarily help run the 2007 festival: what a crazy twist, the same man running two competing festivals – it could only happen in Thailand. Yet to have ousted the American and put our own man in charge is not to scratch exactly where you itch. It is the right move, of course, but there are other factors that need to be put into the equation.

A movie festival should spring from the collective enthusiasm of audiences, film professionals and the government. The shaky Thai film industry, the different factions, cliques and vested interests, and chiefly the fact that the mainstream industry looks down on independent and 'arthouse' filmmakers – these do not constitute a healthy foundation for a solid, expandable film festival. The audience base, too, needs to be broadened to ensure long-term, sustained activities of the festival. Most importantly, the government must realise that they cannot 'buy' a successful movie fest. This implies a larger idea of our country's cultural policy and the role the movies should play in a developing nation struggling to reconcile economic necessity, social values and cultural growth of its people.

Opposition has long demurred that a tourism board is not an ideal host of a movie festival. While that's a difficult point to argue with, it would be particularly tricky for Thailand were BKKIFF transferred to the supervision of a cultural agency, namely the Culture Ministry, known for its conservative attitude and, in certain cases, narrow-mindedness. Without being pessimistic, we can foresee other complications – notably censorship – should the festival be run by the self-styled Thai cultural watchdogs. Thus an alternative must be found. One possible way is for the City of Bangkok to play host, and maybe portions of the finance can come from private sponsors. No structural shake-up, however, seemed likely in the lead up to the 2008 edition, and the TAT looked set to continue to chair the event.

The bribery scandal may have exposed a few corrupt bureaucrats. But beyond that surface crime it also exposes catastrophic consequences of misguided government policies, and perhaps the ease with which greed can exploit the enthusiasm to embrace 'the culture'. There is hope, nevertheless, in the existing Thai Short Film and Video Festival and the World Film Festival of Bangkok. As for BKKIFF, lessons have been learned – hard lessons – and hopefully what happened also means the opportunity for a fresh start. It's important to have faith. Things will get better, I'm certain, because it couldn't possibly get any worse than this.

.

Staus Quo and Beyond: The Viennale, a Success Story

CHRISTOPH HUBER

0. Histories

In the last one-and-a-half decades, Vienna's international film festival, the Viennale, has acquired an outstanding international reputation. It certainly is one of the better festivals of its kind around, but the effusive praise from certain quarters treating the Viennale as some kind of cinephile paradise is just as baffling to me as the damning frustration expressed by friends and acquaintances of all kinds (film critics and filmmakers – especially Austrian ones – as well as regular and casual cinema-goers); some of the criticism seems more than justified, and some of the praise as well. The issues (on both counts) raised in debates about the festival I've had through the years mostly seemed a matter of perspective – and this is not just a question of viewpoints tainted by personal experience or preferences of taste but the festival's standing is also an indicator of a constantly shifting film culture and its blinders internationally, but with some Austrian touches. So I came to the logical conclusion that the best way to tackle this situation is to retrace my relationship to the festival taking place every October on my home turf (I moved to Vienna in 1991, so the period perfectly coincides with its international 'rise'), first as a 'normal' cinephile, then as a professional critic (both periods of roughly equal length). Necessarily and inevitably, at different times the festival has meant different things to me. But what emerges clearly is not just a story of dreams (fulfilled) or disappointments – but a chronicle of changing demands. One could also be tempted to christen this piece, 'Viennese Histoire(s) du cinema', but actually that would make it part of the problem, as we will see.

1. Memories

Try as I might, I cannot remember the first film I saw at Vienna's film festival, although I like to think it was either Tod Browning's immortal *Freaks* or Jean Rouch's equally essential *Les maitres fous* – they might even have been on the same programme. Using the invaluable index of all films played at the festival – 'Viennale – Internationale Filmfestwochen Wien 1960–1996 Registerband' (published by the Festival in 1996; more on it in the second section of this article) – in an attempt to reconstruct my first festival experience, I mostly come up short as well I might; at this point I am an 18-year-old student that has arrived in Vienna a few weeks prior. Up to then, while residing in my small Upper Austrian hometown, my rabidly growing cinephilia had to be nourished mostly via television, certainly not the worst option at that time, when state-sponsored television still did offer programming with a certain cultural responsibility, and not just served up classics, but also stretched into certain margins (even the commercial channels of German-language TV in their early years yielded pleasures high- and lowbrow; with special fondness I remember a near-complete Russ Meyer retrospective productively challenging a Godard anniversary series on state TV in its montage mastery). Since my hometown's cinema was shuttered, monthly screenings by 'cultural initiatives' only furthered my filmic isolation amidst provincial circumstances (I was, on the one hand, not wowed by Jim Jarmusch's jokes – and, on the other hand, one of the few viewers not appalled by Cronenberg's *Dead Ringers*.) Occasionally I could negotiate a drive to a nearby city (their cinema programming mostly wasn't worth it anyway), and the video recorder came too late; it was only acquired months before I left for Vienna. You know you live in the sticks, when, on a very basic level, the move means that you actually might get to see something like *Goodfellas* upon its release.

So basically, in those first months, Vienna's somewhat diverse cinema culture itself is a film festival for me, and it is more of a nice surprise that –

amidst adjusting my life as physics student and cinemagoer – I discover, only very shortly before it's beginning, there is an actual film festival as well. Its two most important aspects back then: the Apollo, the small three-room-multiplex (two of the screens being very small), is close to my dormitory (I tend to get lost easily in the city in the first weeks), and one of my heroes, John Carpenter, is coming in person – he reacts professionally, but very nicely to my timid autograph request. His signature is long lost, like most of my impressions of the festival: I definitely did see some Carpenters on the big screen back then, and discovered Jon Jost, whom the other retrospective is devoted to, but I don't think I watched even one new film (in retrospect it turns out there weren't that many on offer). Most unforgivably, I do not even notice the big historical retrospective on Chinese cinema that is clearly the most sensational aspect of this edition. Glancing into papers, I do take note of some criticisms directed at the festival direction (Reinhard Pyrker and Werner Herzog – yes, *the* Werner Herzog), which sound reasonable enough (doing a Carpenter tribute, how can they omit his rare early western short?), but my concerns are mostly elsewhere.

One year later, a new directorial duo (Wolfgang Ainberger and Alexander Horwath) clearly raises the stakes (with critical and audience success): The contemporary film programme is vastly expanded – as is my intake. It must be close to twenty films in ten days, which is more or less the maximum my studies (and finances) allow, although not nearly enough to form an opinion about the entire festival – not something I would think about then anyway. What is already certain, though, is that this bigger Viennale does have quite a few things on offer that appeal to me, especially in that expedient category slowly starting to take shape in my brain: films that otherwise will not show up in local cinemas. They include Tsukamoto Shinya's remarkable *Tetsuo* films (successfully geared to the audience as instant cult discoveries), but also, more unexpectedly, films I would hardly characterise as offbeat, like Carl Franklin's thriller *One False Move*, for whose regular release I wait for in vain, discovering that the ways of distribution do not necessarily make sense. (Cf. a similar case from that year's line-up, Paul Schrader's *Light Sleeper*, which will show up … quite a few years down the road. An invaluably helpful measure will long have been installed in the festival catalogue by then: an annotation on which films do have distribution.) Films that eventually will play cinemas soon enough (and I have no interest in seeing at the festival anyway) teach me another, quite universal lesson when I foolishly give them a chance during the commerical run: be wary of so-called 'gala screenings' (*Sister Act, 1492*). More insights beginning to dawn: just because some films in a retrospective are relatively easy to come by, other items may not be – a remarkable, big showcase of boxing films is a prime example; by then I am not yet savvy enough to realise that, say, Tod Browning's *The Iron Man* may never show up again (still waiting), whereas the perceived singular opportunity to see Stanley Kubrick's short *Day of the Fight* is misguided since the film proves to be far from a rare item. Similarly, I spend much time at the other retrospective dedicated to the austere art of Robert Bresson (surrounded by selected, 'related' films from Flaherty to Yanagimachi, Garrel and Pialat), assuming all these supposedly difficult works will rarely show up again – when I really should have gorged on the lively shorts featured in the tribute to Les Blank, which have continued to remain elusive.

By 1993, the grasp of film on my life has increased further: actually, starting to present special series throughout the rest of the year (Yugoslavian film, Cassavetes), the Viennale does its best to contribute, but the first time around things do not work out – the showcases take place too close to exam season which I still take very seriously. But during October, when the festival itself takes place, I can by now manage to reshuffle time (and funds) relatively easily, doubling the amount of films towards forty, which will remain constant throughout the next years. Both the festival and I have moved – as the Apollo is rebuilt to become a confusingly huge multiplex, the Viennale spreads around a manageable portion of the inner city (actually into those likeable five cinemas it is still using today). A surge of afternoon screenings helps to expand my selection and widen my interests, which used to tilt (with youthful enthusiasm) towards genre films, the thrillers and fantastic/horror films programmed in appropriate late-night slots. Horwath's (his co-direction with Ainberger lasts till 1994, then he remains in charge alone for two more years) programming credo, tinged with a humorously Austrian tilt described as 'From Arnold (Schwarzenegger) to (Martin) Arnold', i.e. trying to reach from the mainstream to the margin, perfectly fits the bill for me, as I discover new areas. (For instance, the so-called 'avant-garde' has simply been unavailable to me in Upper Austria, save for about five films –

including Arnold's *Pièce touchée* – on television; but Vienna has a strong experimental film culture, with regular screening opportunities, I try to catch up eagerly.) In the next few years, transcendence comes in all forms, from dream retrospectives of known quantities (finally, the complete works of Dario Argento or – small, but endless – Terrence Malick on the big screen in 1993) to hitherto unknown ones (a tribute to Iranian master Bahram Beyzai in 1995 also putting the then-emerging craze for Iranian cinema into perspective). I begin to appreciate the interplay of the old and the new and learn to accept that it can be meaningful by default (as in the Beyzai case) or sheer accident: Arthur Aristakisjan's epic *Ladoni* literally leaves me speechless, as it is unlike anything I've ever seen – then again, so is another black-and-white mindfuck, Suzuki Seijun's long-awaited classic *Branded to Kill*, finally making its way over here with Dutch subtitles only, with some slightly incomprehensible results that perfectly enhance its surrealism.

The Viennale screened Suzuki Seijun's *Branded to Kill* with Dutch subtitles

There are (and always have been and always will be) disappointments as well, but by now I'm beginning to develop a sense of perspective: it dawns on me that the idea of a festival cannot just be the discussion of a single film, which is the usual distraction when it comes down to classify a festival, whether in attack or defense – for in the end what is it worth to weigh the time wasted in, say, Hal Hartley's *Amateur* against the ecstatic two hours of Kumashiro Tatsumi's *Hard-Headed Fool*? The question rather has to be: what context is created for these two? (Are they surrounded by more waste or by more ecstasy?) The point of context is brought home painfully when the Viennale's extraneous summer retrospective dedicated to Hong Kong cinema of the 1980s and 1990s turns out to be a premiere-heavy revelation – yet the foreword to the programme bafflingly extols the films' virtues as mostly no-brains entertainment. On the other hand, Horwath's two big consecutive Viennale retrospectives in 1994 and 1995 – dedicated to innovative Hollywood cinema from 1960–68 and 1967–75 respectively – are like provocative seminars on the presentation of film history; being familiar with big parts of the selection from television, new perspectives arise not just from being able to finally revisit them on the big screen (and in original versions; after all TV is firmly in the hands of a sadly dubbed film culture), but also from rarer works surrounding them and encountered for the first time. That I agree on most, but not necessarily all of the selections, has instructive results: I must learn to formulate my objections within a broader system of ideas. (Of course it is still true that Roger Vadim's *Barbarella* is plain ridiculous, but how does that ridiculousness fit into the proposed scheme of things?)

A key year comes in 1996: first, the retrospectives remind how the sense of film history is shaped by the status quo. Following up on his Hollywood excursions, Horwath concludes his tenure with a huge and hugely enjoyable series on 1930s films, 'Before the Code'; much is to be discovered, but I also realise that I know a lot more here than I did from the big 'Nouvelle Vague' showcase in May (curated by Frieda Grafe); and I already knew a lot more of that, than I did of the cinema of Werner Hochbaum, an extraordinary, unsung director working in the 1930s, in Germany – and Austria. The Hochbaum retrospective (in March) is actually a reprise of a deserving Viennale programme from 1976, reinforcing the sense of how film history is shaped. After all, I have hardly heard of the major director working in my country at the same time as those Hollywood films were made, with whose (hi) stories and creators I'm so familiar. It would be interesting to have a similar perspective on the contemporary selection, I think, especialy since Vienna's film festival has found both audience success and international reputation under Horwath's direction: for me his 1996 tribute selection – Olivier Assayas & André Téchiné, Mike Leigh & Ken Loach – is a welcome chance to delve into oeuvres so far only visible in spots (and with Assayas, for instance, only through the Viennale itself) in Austria. But given the acclaimed status of these directors as Euro-Giants, what does it mean internationally? Not to mention the contemporary selection, for which the frame of reference in those pre-internet-days is just a puny assortment of festival reports in the Austrian papers and articles from a handful of overpriced international film magazines. One would have to go to those festivals oneself, I conclude – but I go to Linz, to finish my diploma thesis in the Voest steel works. Horwath's last gift before he hands the festival over to Hans Hurch (who is still in charge and will be at least a few more years) is a perfect *vade mecum* for more historical thought – the index of all Viennale editions up to then.

2. Fantasies

In those ten years I've spent with the Viennale index, my perspective on it has changed as well: back then it was full of mysterious names, with classics or at least established works thrown in for good measure. I have encountered quite a bit of once seemingly enigmatic works since, but the allure of the unknown remains. Of course, on paper, the potential of festivals is always greater – unencumbered by necessities or even simple scheduling conflicts the attractive stands out (a first look at a festival's programme is always more promising than the final result) – and the eccentric is just charming. I haven't counted the numbers, but for instance it seems that Italian animation artist Bruno Bozzetto may be the secret favorite of Viennale: the alphabetical order of the listings even twice brings up the intiguing progression Bozzetto; Bresson (followed by Michael Cacoyannis in 1971; by Claude Chabrol in 1974). Wedged in between, 1973 yields the second return to the festival programme for Loach, Ermanno Olmi and Ephraim Kishon. In short, the selection criteria remain intriguingly obscure. The first year of the Viennale gives a reasoning in its title ('Films That Did Not Reach Us'), and characteristically ranges from the great (Sergei Bondarchuck, Kurosawa Akira) to the overrated (Camus' *Orfeu negro*) to the forgotten and obscure (who is Gyula Macskassy?) For a few years in the mid-1960s the Viennale reconceives itself as a 'Festival of exhilaration', visibly favouring a certain amount of 'quality' comedies, but including – I randomly pick 1964 – a selection from Ozu Yasujiro's farewell to Vera Chytilova's (feature) debut to arcane Bulgarian works (one title, by Boika Mawrodinowa, is given in literal translation as *Pedagogic Poem*). By 1968 there is a return to serious assignments, first reprising the 'Films That Did Not Reach Us' moniker, but quickly upping the didactic ante towards the likes of 'Inconvenient Contemporaries'; remarkable is the year 1970 ('Society and Young Generation') for its focus on 'new Austrian cinema', including a big retrospective dedicated to the movement's tenth anniversary. Apart from two years in the late 1970s which have a special sidebar ('Cannes in Vienna'), the selection preferences, with or without a moniker, seem stimulatingly inscrutable – is even most of it coming from the big festivals, like so much is today? Various emphases throughout the years (more Eastern Europe here, a Dutch Defilée there) seem to be traces of personal preferences by the directors. A perfect starting point to consider the Hurch era after noting two more facts, both still pertinent: from early on the Viennale has striven to enrich its programme by historical retrospectives, and that they have consistently grown over the years is certainly a good thing. As is Hurch's steadfast dedication to keeping the festival in the inner city cinemas, which is an integral part of the festival's distinct flair – and which, as I discovered thanks to the index, was not a move in 1993, but a return: all of the cinemas (and a few that no longer exist) had been Viennale venues throughout its history, the Apollo was just an interlude coinciding with my arrival.

3. Realities

My arrival at Hurch's Viennale is just two prolonged weekends out of the Voest, mostly well spent at the tribute to Albert Brooks and the big retrospective of Roberto Rossellini. So, in 1997, I have little reason to join in with many complaints that the Viennale is hardly a festival of exhilaration anymore, despite continuing audience success: Hurch follows the established formula, which has made the Viennale a cultural event (also meaning many attend without *really* caring what they see; as always – but that is true with every festival – prestige productions, scheduled to open soon are always sold out first). That Hurch's proclivities lie somewhere else is showing throughout the years: Francophilia, but especially a preference for documentary (and realist) modes tip the scales, while the mainstream balance feels rather more dutiful than enthusiastic – and the selection of genre films has been, to say it politely, erratic. (I sometimes ask myself how my younger self, that responded so enthusiastically once, would react a mere decade later; certainly with more indifference.) The director's penchant for antagonising helps little, even if after a few years press coverage goes the way of the Austrian solution, mainly – much ballyhoo in advance, hardly any stocktaking afterwards; at one press conference Hurch announces that if he would really make a festival for himself he would play ten movies at most, which overplays the 'inconvenient contemporary' card to the point of disdain for the audience. His often contentious relationship to Austrian cinema has been an issue as well: at another press conference (they are beginning to sound a lot more interesting than they are) he pointed out that the meagre two Austrian fiction features he selected were actually quite bad. Although the Austro-numbers have somewhat increased (albeit still far below what Horwath presented), the residual resentment of the local film community is understandable, especially since there would be an easy solution at hand – i.e. freeing Austrian films from the Viennale regulation that new films have to be Austrian premieres (many of which premier earlier that year at the Austrian film festival in Graz – but some of the best do not make it to Vienna's screens).

Yet these are problems that matter little to the international standing of the Viennale, and in part that is understandable; I certainly lived through a similar period of disillusionment after starting to write on film more or less professionally shortly after my return to Vienna in 1998 and soon starting to travel to other festivals. If previously, the Viennale had been my most important, in some cases only chance to see certain films, now I could easily catch up with those elsewhere – or had already seen them in advance. (Meanwhile other festivals, like Torino before its 2007 takeover, served as replacement to gorge on really heady programming.) It would be easy to bicker about this or that selection, but that would mostly just be gamesmanship. However, it is worth noting that as a self-proclaimed audience festival, the small amount of what you could classify as excellent genre filmmaking, or at least good entertainment, is somewhat frustrating. And, alas, the festival has mostly moved away from presenting premieres (ah, to think of Eiichi Kudo's towering goodbye *Gunro no keifu* in 1998), with haphazard, even clumsy attempts to compensate with strict festival filler (*Double Vision*), while ignoring even circuit-approved masters like Takashi Miike (save, alas again, for *One Last Call*), and dare I even mention non-approved ones ones like Cheang Soi-pou?

More generally frustrating is a strange lack of consequence: not diligently following up on filmmakers (for example, Jacques Rivette, Aoyama Shinji) who have received tributes or have been the subject of retrospectives, although the Viennale screening would clearly be the only chance of Austrian exposure. Hurch may have complaints about Rivette's *Histoire de Marie et Julien* (I can't comment, as its no-show at Viennale is one of the reasons I still haven't seen it), but can it be much inferior to Rivette's incredibly overrated *Va savoir*, the preceding film from the year that warranted the retrospective? Locally, Hurch's dedication to the work of Danièle Huillet and Jean-Marie Straub has been the butt of many jokes, but I find it touching not just because it is deserved, but precisely because it goes to such ridiculous lengths as showing an undistinguished TV biography of Fritz Lang ostensibly just because Straub utters a few sentences in it. Yet the only other person warranting this sort of enshrinement is Jean-Luc Godard – and here I see, in a nutshell, the embodiment of the international reputation of the festival: Godard is *the* offical icon, with Straub doubling as his doppelganger for the more radically predisposed – the last stand of film as we know it. This is the emblematic status quo of a serious cinephilia behind which lurks a 1960s/1970s conception of cinema that is, often unwittingly, idolised today, and the Viennale caters to it – certainly not cynically, I'm sure, but by predisposition. Actually most of the tributes carry the stamp of that era, whether it's rediscoveries *du jour* (Peter Whitehead, Danny Williams) or eternal wisdom (Hartmut Bitomsky, Emile de Antonio). Indeed, even the documentary selection the Viennale prides itself for tends to reflect a bias for TV fodder once a music or film icon from the era is involved as a subject. Even though usually leavened by a welcome tribute to a current art-house filmmaker of interest (Koreeda Hirokazu, Pedro Costa) and a tribute to Hollywood greats (from Dean Martin to Fay Wray or Lauren Bacall – the latter two even brought a different kind of glamour to the festival) that mitigates the dearth of entertainment, it all seems quite predictable, right down to the mediocrity of the Chinese selection and discoveries from American avant-garde circles that include Viennale mainstays James Benning, Thom Andersen, and John Gianvito. The latter may even be the year's best *(Los Angeles Plays Itself, Profit Motive and the Whispering Wind)*, along with some retrospectives (especially since the film archive has joined in with bigger series from Paul Fejos to proletarian cinema in the last years), but overall there is a lack of surprise – no threat that, even despite its quotes from experimental filmmaking, something like the crypto-CalArts porn *Art School Sluts* might be juxtaposed with the school's own work, or Nando Cicero, the demented Straub of Italian sex comedy, might be programmed alongside the 'sane', serious Straub. There have been some enjoyable nutty ideas recently – a showcase for Buenos Aires on film in a moving gesture of solidarity for just-fired Buenos Aires film fest director Quintín, a random selection of 'jungle' movies – but a feeling remains that all the excellence, whether past or present, is not really challenged by the truly innovative. Of course, these choices doubtless makes the Viennale easier to like – in addition to the fact that its programme is still vastly better than that of most comparable festivals and does show a personal touch.

Hurch even seems to occasionally acknowledge his weaknesses by making an effort to outsource showcases with outstanding results; recent examples include a midnight movies selection by Munich specialists of the 'Werkstattkino', the rich retrospectives on 'Blacklisted' films curated by Thom Andersen and Noel Burch, Roland Domenig's survey of Japan's 'Art Theatre Guild' and – most recently – Jean-Pierre Gorin's selection of 'essay films'. Yet 2007 also drove home some of the festival's limitations: instead of an actress of old Hollywood along came another 1960s/1970s icon, Jane Fonda, to professionally spread glamour and wow the nostalgists. Unfortunately, the tribute films added little of note to the overall quality of the programming (beyond an opportunity to see the rarity *Introduction to the En-*

Jean Renoir's *This Land is Mine* was featured in a tribute to Maureen O'Hara at the Viennale

emy), the strain of Fonda's 'committed' projects actually quite the opposite of the (no less committed) effortless entertainments that starred honorees like Maureen O'Hara or Olivia de Havilland (just contrast *Coming Home* with *This Land is Mine* or *Barefoot in the Park* with *The Strawberry Blonde*; also, no contrast needed: *Barbarella* again). More intriguingly and tellingly, Gorin's mostly delectable selection ranged through the whole of cinema – but the basis of its argument again marked a reversion to the myths of the 1960s, in this case the idea of *cinéma vérité* as orthodox interpretation of the documentary form; only in relation to this aesthetic filter could some films be elevated (mostly from the documentary genre) to the status of essays. But as with most of the programming, the spectator had to make the effort to be challenged. As at other noteworthy festivals, critical thinking and creative ferment is possible at the Viennale although the event does not require viewers to adopt a critical stance per se.

Bagatelle for Kino Otok and i 1000 Occhi

OLAF MÖLLER

Izola/Isola and Trieste/Trst are about twenty minutes by car apart, a border – of politico-historically confused as well as culturally vaguer character – has to be crossed on the way. Izola is a tiny fishing village, right next to Koper/Capo d'Istria, the main city on the forty kilometres of coastline belonging to the westernmost Slavic country, Slovenia. Trieste, however, is the easternmost major city of Italy, a true harbour town architecturally defined during the Austro-Hungarian Empire. In addition, both places belong to that part of the Adriatic where civilisations met and merged: officially, the region is bilingual – Italian and Slovene – with German as an unofficial third tongue. Reading Italo Svevo – a core Triestinian with a love for German – in the original will give you an idea of the region's linguistic idiosyncrasies, its particular nature. At its most generous, it's international – in ways ever rarer in our globalised era.

Both places also host film festivals of quite uncommon character: Izola Kino Otok (= Cinema Island), Trieste i 1000 occhi (= the thousand eyes). While Kino Otok is seemingly the only major cultural event in sleepy lovely Izola, i 1000 occhi is but one of about half a dozen film festivals which take place over the year in Trieste. Both are comparatively new adventures: i 1000 occhi was founded in 2002 by Sergio Grmek Germani and Mila Lazic, Kino Otok two years on by Vlado Skafar, who was succeeded by Koen van Daele. In their own ways, both are also very young festivals. And

An open-air cinema at the Kino Otok festival. (photo: Tina Smrekar)

rather small ones: Kino Otok takes place over the course of just five days in late May/early June, in three venues – one an improvised open-air cinema smack in the village's centre – showing a total of something like thirty films or programmes; i 1000 occhi happens for eight days in late September, in just one venue, featuring give or take forty programmes. What's remarkable in the case of Kino Otok is that (at least) parts of its programme are usually reprised just a day or so later in Ljubljana, the capital, which is roughly an hour by car away; keep in mind Slovenia is a tiny country with a small population and one would suspect that the screenings in Ljubljana might become a problem for the main event. But they don't; Kino Otok is as much about the cinephile community by the beach as it is for the films that get shown.

That said, neither Kino Otok nor i 1000 occhi thinks of itself as small; they're not Small Festivals, those passive-aggressive pests whose sense of self is defined mainly in negative terms, by not being big, not being important, not featuring any major premieres, stars, whathaveyou, by showing more or less only Small – instead of Big, Major, Important – films usually by 'underappreciated' or 'over-looked' directors, etc., and always, always with an emphasis on being for the audience, by which they mean the viewer as semi-refined consumer; festivals which define themself only in relationship to some status quo, happy in their little niche or corner, content with being an eternal, ankle-biting complementary attraction. Kino Otok and i 1000 occhi are nothing like that: each of them has a distinctive raison d'etre and they're not parasitic upon other festivals.

Both are also conscious experiments in co-dependence, Kino Otok in particular: it is part of an informal association of similarly interested and sized international festivals with which they sometimes share prints and travel expenses, occasionally develop programming ideas etc. Things here function on a solidarity basis. Programme-wise, both festivals stubbornly refuse facile pigeonholing: they reconsider and reinvent themselves edition by edition. Let's say they're developing festivals.

On the surface, Kino Otok looks like the more orthodox of the two: it mainly shows recent films yet unpremiered in Slovenia, with a focus on Asian, African, South-and-Central American, as well as Central-and-Eastern European cinemas – call it an adventure in de-othering; it even has a miniscule competition. Now, making the festival meant for all involved learning what kind of festival they actually wanted to make, and therewith what they wanted from cinema and therefore life. And what became ever clearer is that as far as the festival's essence is concerned, soul has less to do with the origins of the films than with the attitude with which they're made. Meaning Kino Otok is about that which Werner Herzog's *The Wild Blue Yonder* (2005), Matthew Barney's *Drawing Restraint 9* (2005), Lav Diaz's *Heremias* (2006), Zelimir Zilnik's *Evropa preko plota* (2005) and Wakamatsu Koji's *17-sai no fukei – Shonen wa nani o mita no ka* (2004) have in common – that anarchistic freedom, sense of wonder, that desire to (be)come frame by frame, moment to moment, that existential need for intellectual/spiritual growth. Cinema as celebration.

Part of Kino Otok's sense of self was always pedagogical: the event exemplifies, in as practical a manner as possible, what cinema can be. Since 2006, it even includes a (sort-of) school: a cycle of screenings and lectures in memory of Silvan Furlan, the founder and first director of the Slovenian Cinematheque – nothing too formal, but done in such a way that people can actually learn something. The presence of older films and directors – always only a few, chosen/invited with great care and deliberation – feels therefore somewhat different here than at most other places: its about handing on things.

The festival's mainly for Slovenes, while foreigners are a more than welcomed part of it – they'll find their way if they want to, and do so in ever greater numbers – the visitors as well as the crew are very young, somewhere in their late twenties. There's a mess patio for all participants, right behind Kino Otok's camping ground, close to Punta, a patch of meadow by the sea where the nights never grow old (just ask Lisandro Alonso). People constantly meet – Izola is tiny, all the festival spaces are close to each other – everything is relaxed, despite six screenings per day for the true cinephages.

And let's not forget the football match, the one thing for which the hungriest movie muncher is willing to forget about films for an hour or two. Kino Otok-regulars talk about this months before the festival even begins. Legend has it that the festival was only founded for the football match (which is not true but a great story), and that sometimes the films are selected by their maker's reputed skills with a ball (which does happen). Strange things were sighted on the pitch, like a Kazakh director storming with a water bottle in his hand. Asked long after the festival about his memories of Izola, Roger Gnoan M'Bala started to talk passionately about refereeing the first-ever Kino Otok-match. Wrists and knees got injured last time. It was worth it, certainly.

Usually the sun shines bright, and beauty rules. It's an atmosphere where filmmakers are willing to talk for hours and people listen attentively, making Kino Otok into something like a symposium disguised as a film festival. The event is the community.

Something similar can be said about i 1000 occhi, its merry, little by little expanding band of brothers and sisters in cinema. Quite impossible to pigeonhole as it is, 'format'-wise: it's in no way about recent films but it doesn't mind them, they happen and belong, although the majority of works shown are of earlier vintages; it's not a festival of retrospectives even if they make up the major part of the programme. It's not about looking back but about how one looks at them now, the instant of rememberance-recognition; and it's not about a particular genre or region or period, for everything can find its place here. Looking at i 1000 occhi's inaugural edition, the auteurs in focus then – Jean Vigo, Jose Val del Omar, Victor Erice, Alexis Damianos and Massimo Troisi – all iconoclasts creating at their own pace – one might say that the festival is about cinema as a way of life which at times takes manifest stock in artistic deeds; some, like Jess Franco or Terence Fisher (later in the fifth edition) hemorrhage films while others just occasion them.

i 1000 occhi embodies an instantaneous way of writing film history, a process of on-going research into the nature of cinema, its development and all of its complex, perplexing vastness. The festival is guided by the spirit of neorealism as personified by Roberto Rossellini – the award the festival inaugurated three years ago honouring the life-time achievement of *un cineasta del nostro tempo* side-tracked by the discourses of these days – recepients in recent years include Mircea Daneliuc, Werner Schroeter, Paulo Rocha – is named after the master's last feature film, *Anno uno*.

Sergio Grmek Germani's programming also shows that one doesn't need to dig around in cinema's stranger corners to come up with something surprising: it all depends on vision, which in Germani's case is totally partisan – in days when the dominant discourse is that of collaborators, those who make do, and too often mere cowards and compromisers.

The history written here – better still, the presence defined – is a very personal one: it's the cinema as seen, experienced, thought about, enjoyed, considered and reconsidered by Germani, as well as Mila Lazic. Their histories – as festival programmers and consultants, critics, students of cinema, and makers of films – are the driving force of i 1000 occhi. A good part of the festival's programming is rooted in, and references, work already done – like the monumental retrospectives for Trieste's Alpe Adria (Yugoslav Black Wave; a Croatian Cinema apart; a certain Romanian Cinema), or Torino (Stavros Tornes, and so forth), or Venice (for example Andrzej Munk) – also to old friendships, to visits and meetings and presents, to memories. Departed colleagues, teachers, inspirations are remembered, usually in surprising ways: when the critic Alberto Farassino, one of the kindest and most generous representatives of Italian film culture, died in 2003, i 1000 occhi mourned this friend's passing by showing an hour-long TV-essay in montage on Luis Buñuel – a life-long obsession of Farassino – which he assembled in 1980 together with Tatti Sanguinetti, plus Nando Cicero's *Ultimo tango a Zagarol* (1973), a brusquely vulgar parody of Bertolucci's wannabe classic of bourgeois pulp, satirising the falseness and pretentiousness in the characteristic Cicero manner. This combination perfectly encapsulated the ever-surprising inquisitive and iconoclastic spirit of Farassino, as well as the enthusiasm which made him such an indispensable component of i 1000 occhi. When Germani featured the recently deceased Paduan film collector and all-round cinephile Piero Tortolina as an artistic consultant for the sixth i 1000 occhi – mind: post mortem! – it was a beautiful and well chosen expression of gratitude, as well of how we live with the departed, their essences, lessons; and now contemplate the quiet genius of the films shown in memoriam: Giacomo Gentilomo's *Ecco la radio!* (1940), of which Tortolina owned the only existing print, flanked by a *fuori orario*-documentary about Gentilomo, arguably the most interesting filmmaker from Trieste, featuring a short appearance by Tortolina, and finally another Tortolina-rarity, a 16mm-print of the Italian dub of Jacques Becker's *Le Trou* (1960) which is slightly different from the French original as well as the general Italian release version.

It's in these cases that the particular nature of i 1000 occhi's catalogues comes most strongly to the fore: these ever-thicker publications are no mere one-movie-one/two-page-summary+cast-&-credits+director's filmography-affairs but highly personal collections of pictures and essays – super partisan at times – adding depth and further heart to the festival's general experience; just take the beautiful piece on certain treasures of Italian film history in dire need of digging out (again) – quite a few with a cine/real-politically 'complex' history – and on the necessity of providing adequate prints to present/preserve them, a propos *La citta' dolente* (1949) by Mario Bonnard (and Enrico Morelli) presented at the fourth i 1000 occhi; or, one edition later, a few choice thoughts *a propos* Mikhail Romm's *Obyknovennyi fashizm* (*Ordinary Fascism*, 1965) and the films of Sergei Gerasimov – the cinema of a country, the Soviet Union, that no longer exists and the contradictory genius of directors who were able to combine 'orthodoxy' and freedom – simple observations, perhaps, although reflections of this kind sometimes have quite a liberating effect.

Poster for the 2004 edition of
the i 1000 occhi festival

Continuity is one of the keys to i 1000 occhi: things here are rarely done with in one edition, they gestate; more often than not, names and titles appear and re-appear, finding ever-new meanings in ever-different contexts. The fifth i 1000 occhi, for example, offered the opportunity to see a double-feature of Rossellini's *Anima nera* and Dino Risi's *Il sorpasso*, both from 1962: the former something of a rarity considered a failure in its days, the latter an era-defining masterpiece; the films opened one right after the other in some cinemas. *Anima nera* went and *Il sorpasso* came; seen like this together (*Il sorpasso*'s melancholia, *Anima nera*'s sardonic grating) the two become a dyptich about the discontent and pain at the heart of the Italy of the economic miracle. Or take the third i 1000 occhi: alongside the mind-boggling double-bill of Saw Teong *Hin's Puteri gunung Ledang* (2004) and Rossellini's *Un pilota ritorna* (1942) – programme title: da Rossellini a Rossellini – it takes some serious grace to think that one up. The festival, upping the ante some more, also presented Larisa Shepitko's *Kryl'ja* (1966), as a teaser for the Shepitko retrospective, which was finally presented two years later: three films about the dream of flying; three distinct yet different relationships to time and history, between legend and propaganda and reality, nations and their (un) making; three essays on a possible essence of cinema.

Probably the drollest i 1000 occhi regular is Nando Cicero, the Straub of erotic comedies: he pops up every other year, in 2007 like a Jack-in-the-box on closing night when his debut *Le scippo* (1966) was shown as a farewell surprise film; what a marvelous obsession.

It takes guts to start a film festival that isn't hellbent on being some mega-event or a new player on the market, a festival that doesn't see itself as but another link in the exploitation chain, i 1000 occhi could have just as well been gone after its first year – the 2003 event was called Edizione di Emergenza – in Italian, as in English, the last word's related to emergence – something which the festival's masters and commanders were able to prevent through careful manoevering – while getting ever more radical in their programming.

Recently, because of the ever greater chaos in Slovene film culture after the last election, in which the right wing ascended to power, the very existence of Kino Otok became imperiled. The festival found itself under fire because of an increasingly absurd series of events. The National Film Board sent a letter to the festival with the grandiose statement that Kino Otok was an extremely important cultural event and therefore worthy of maximum subsidy – and then offered half the amount usually given to the festival. When Kino Otok pointed this out to the people in power, they duly received another letter which stated that, on second glance, the festival is actually irrelevant and won't receive any grant money at all. The festival didn't take place in 2008. Plans for 2009 – when this pernicious government will be, with any luck, finally ousted – have been made.

Presences like Kino Otok or i 1000 occhi, which insist on the importance of art for our development and growth as human beings, are beginning to seem increasingly unreal. Both exist in the constant shadow of extinction: they are infinitely expendable since the wealth they create is primarily cultural.

Some Festivals I've Known: A Few Rambling Recollections

JONATHAN ROSENBAUM

I'm pretty sure the first film festival I ever attended was the third New York Film Festival, at age 22 in fall 1965, to see *Alphaville*. In 1963, I probably would have attended the first New York Film Festival if I hadn't transferred from Washington Square College to Bard College, two hours up the Hudson, about half a year earlier. Later that same year, I took over the Friday night film series at Bard, but every once in a while I'd forego one of my own selections in order to take a weekend trip to New York and see something new I was especially curious about; my first looks at *Muriel* and *Dr. Strangelove* were during two such excursions. And my curiosity about what Jean-Luc Godard would do with science fiction was enough to persuade me to hop on the train or catch a ride with a classmate. As it turned out, I found the film silly, not really understanding most of its allusions to contemporary Paris or German expressionist cinema. Taking the movie as 'straight' SF, or at least trying to, made me only slightly more appreciative than John Simon would have been, and I emerged from the screening thinking it was something akin to warmed-over Huxley or Orwell.

On the other hand, this was my first visit to the recently built Lincoln Center, and the way that Alice Tully Hall's lobbies and stairways reflected some of the movie's creepier and glossier architecture momentarily left a

Jonathan Rosenbaum at the Valdivia Film Festival in Chile

more favorable impression. (It wasn't until a few years later, while watching an English-dubbed version of the film on late-night TV, while stoned on grass with a friend, that I started to appreciate the movie in earnest, sensually as well as intellectually.)

In fact, the only film festival I can recall attending in the 1960s was the annual one at the Lincoln Center. Over the next couple of years, while suffering through the pedantic rituals of graduate school on Long Island in order to continue my draft-dodging, I even did some festival coverage for the college newspaper in order to get press credentials, reviewing, among other things, Godard's *Masculine Feminine* and *Made in USA*, Rossellini's *The Rise of Louis XIV*, Skolimowski's *Le départ*, and the multiple-authored *Far from Vietnam* (a particular *cause celèbre* which in some ways made the strongest impression – though it's barely remembered today except as a period curiosity).

As I subsequently discovered in 1968 and 1969, when I didn't write any festival reviews, getting press accreditation for the New York Film Festival in those days was a fairly simple and straightforward matter. By this time, I was already edging my way out of graduate school, now that being both 25 and from Alabama (where enlistments in the military were relatively common) enabled me to feel safer from the threat of being drafted. I was also beginning to become more professionally involved with film criticism because an entrepreneurial friend had hired me to edit a collection called *Film Masters* (a book that led me to postpone some of the work on my second novel for the better part of a year, though like both my novels it never wound up in print). And being part of the festival's freebie crowd at press screenings gave me a pleasant sense of belonging that I tended to take for granted back then.

The same thing was true at the Cannes Film Festival the first time I attended, in May 1970 – having by then moved to Paris from New York the previous fall. All I had to do to get a press card was use some printed stationary belonging to a nonexistent publisher produced by a New York friend for other purposes – the same friend who'd hired me to edit *Film Masters* and then had sold it as a package to McGraw-Hill – and invent a magazine I'd supposedly be writing my coverage for. The following year, however, the Cannes press office was onto my deception and demanded something more real and verifiable. Fortunately, I'd already started to write for the *Village Voice* by then, about my brief adventures as an extra on Robert Bresson's *Four Nights of a Dreamer*, and wound up doing my coverage for them the next two years in a row, after which I managed to write about the festival for *Film Comment* and London's *Time Out* in 1973. (The only glitch in 1971 was that Amos Vogel got the same assignment from a different *Voice* editor. Once we discovered that neither of us had an exclusive beat, we sorted out the films between us and wrote separate articles.)

Mythically and practically, my first year at the Cannes festival was what finally edged me into the outer edges of the Paris film world, because I wound up meeting more people there in ten days than I'd met in Paris during half a year. One of the first of these was Carlos Clarens, a Cuban film critic whom I immediately recognised on the Croisette from having seen him play himself in Agnès Varda's *Lions Love* – a mixture of documentary and fiction about Hollywood hippies that I'd seen at the New York Film Festival in 1969. When I introduced myself, I believe he was en route to his second viewing of *Woodstock* that day, having already attended a press screening that morning.

My own first look at *Woodstock*, a memorable experience, was in the festival's Grand Palais, which was then directly across the street from the Hotel Carlton. Michael Wadleigh, the hippie director – a tall, commanding figure dressed in suede – dedicated the film to the four students killed by National Guardsmen at Kent State only five days earlier, and to 'the many deaths to come', I recall he added. When the screening was over, he stood by the exit and calmly handed out black arm bands to anyone who wanted one. I wore one myself for a day or two, but Warner Bros. was giving out *Woodstock* buttons at the same time, and after a while it began to seem that the arm bands and the buttons were virtually interchangeable; after all, this was Cannes. Then, by the end of the week, as if to prove the point, some boutiques in Cannes started selling black arm bands.

★ ★ ★

Virtually all film festivals can be placed in two functional categories – those that mainly exist in order to facilitate seeing movies and those that mainly exist in order to facilitate selling movies – and New York and Cannes offered me respective paradigmatic examples of each. It doesn't follow from this, however, that those dedicated more to seeing films are necessarily any more sophisticated in terms of either their press or their audiences. If I had to single out two festivals where the herdlike reactions of both reviewers and the public tend to be the most philistine, New York and Cannes could easily fit the bill. The only time in my life when I've ever heard a Robert Breer animated short booed was at a New York Film Festival press screening, and Manny Farber and Patricia Patterson have made apt sport (in their piece about the 1975 New York Film Festival) of the kind of hostility routinely provoked there by 'difficult' films. ("'Is it Ms. Duras' intention to bore the audience, and, if so, does she feel she has succeeded?'") And the noisy, petulant walkouts I recall in Cannes during screenings of *Dead Man* and *The Neon Bible* in the 1990s – or the standing ovations at Cannes that greeted certain moments in *Electra Glide in Blue* in 1973 – are no less emblematic. And sometimes the herdlike behavior of the press at Cannes was merely a matter of what everyone chose to see. I recall being somewhat taken aback in 1973 that I was the only one I knew who decided to attend a low-profile screening – apparently the first in the West – of Teinosuke Kinugasa's recently rediscovered and mind-boggling *A Page of Madness* from 1926 rather than a Palais screening of John Frankheimer's *Impossible Object*.

I can no longer remember which years in Cannes I first met Todd McCarthy and David Overbey, two important early contacts. But I do recall that this happened in Todd's case during his junior year abroad at Stanford, when he was based somewhere in England, and that David, a former English professor, by this time had already moved to Paris from California, where he was living with one of his former students, who worked for UNESCO. This was before Todd went to work for *Variety* (after a similar but briefer stint at *The Hollywood Reporter*) and David became a programmer for what was then called the Toronto Festival of Festivals, both of which occurred in the mid-1970s. These friendships were characteristic of the kinds of links with fellow cinephiles that could be forged at Cannes. (Another key meeting was a casual conversation with Susan Sontag, whom I'd already known since her *Partisan Review* days in the early 1960s, that sparked the only script conference I've ever attended [in Paris, a short time afterwards] – when she showed some momentary interest in directing a screenplay based on J. G. Ballard's *The Crystal World* that I was then writing for a Paris producer, Edith Cottrell.)

I also can recall my amusement at sometimes seeing the entire selection committee of the New York Film Festival at certain Cannes screenings – a group that typically consisted of Richard Roud, Andrew Sarris, Molly Haskell, Susan Sontag, and/or one or two others – walk out of the films in question *en masse*, as if they all had not only identical tastes but also precisely the same burnout points. (Part of the amusement I felt, rightly or wrongly, was at the way some of these people, New Yorkers especially, seemed to cling to one another compulsively at Cannes in mutually protective ways.) There was something mysterious and inscrutable to me back then about some of their taste-making decisions, and it wasn't until I became a member of this committee myself in the years 1994–97, thereby allowing me to resume my attendance at Cannes, that I started to understand some of the practical logistics of that group. During the early 1970s, I was usually dismayed to discover that the committee seemed to opt for selecting films that already had US distributors; it was only during the 1990s that I discovered that I was sometimes mistaken about the chronology – that many of these films on the contrary acquired US distributors *because* they'd been selected by the New York Film Festival. Also, though I don't recall ever sitting together with all the other committee members at any Cannes screenings, I did become more aware of some of the everyday teamlike duties and processes – such as the fact that we all stayed at the Splendid, a small but relatively deluxe hotel that was conveniently close to the newer version of the Palais (a few blocks down the Croisette from the old one), and often had breakfast meetings together there at 7:15 am before attending the first press screenings at 7:45. I also became aware that the more difficult part of the selection process was the marathon viewing sessions held in New York in early August. (My hotel room, virtually across the street from The Lincoln Center, always had a VCR, and typically – after a twelve-hour stint of watching films, interrupted only by a leisurely lunch – I'd be given a few videos to take back to my room as 'homework'. After a while, it became easier for me to perceive how the New York Film Festival could have passed – or subsequently would pass – on such major masterpieces as *A Brighter Summer Day*, *The Aesthenic Sydrome* and *Inquietude*, as well as apparently all the features of such major filmmakers as Pere Portabella and Pedro Costa. Working in such conditions of daily sensory and intellectual overload, the surprising thing was that committee members were able to function critically at all.)

One cherished memory I have of Cannes during the 1970s was a movie theatre called Le Français that no longer exists today, where the films of the Directors' Fortnight were shown. This was a series that, if I'm not mistaken, was launched in 1969 as a kind of alternative venue to the festival's main events in the Palais, and in those days this was still a distinction that meant a great deal. Relatively 'noncommercial' films at the Palais were few and far between – a rare exception was Jean Eustache's 210-minute *La maman et la putain* in 1973 – so most of the edgier fare that I saw there in that period was at Le Français, including such items as *Aguirre, the Wrath of God*, *Brother Carl*, *How Tasty Was My Little Frenchmen*, *Othon*, *Punishment Park*, *Valparaiso, Valparaiso!*, *WR: Mysteries of the Organism*, and two particular oddball favorites, *Vampir-Cuadacuc* and *Some Call It Loving*. Best of all, there was a bar in this cinema with a large plate-glass window enabling me to glimpse random samples of a film while eating a sandwich and thereby determine whether to return to see the whole thing later.

★ ★ ★

Apart from New York and Cannes, I can almost count the other film festivals I attended during the 1970s on one hand: San Sébastian in 1972; London in 1974–76 (after moving to London to work for the British Film Institute, as assistant editor of the *Monthly Film Bulletin*); Edinburgh in 1975 and 1976 (which I covered both years for *Sight and Sound*); Filmex in Los Angeles in 1977–78 (after I moved from London to San Diego, to teach film at the

University of California); the Toronto Festival of Festivals, thanks to David Overbey, in 1978; and Venice, to attend a three-day conference called 'The Cinema in the 80s', in 1979.

The San Sébastian bash, held back then in July, was by far the glitziest – an event that incorporated not only a good many midnight banquets at country clubs, but also a trip to Pamplona to attend the bullfight, with Howard Hawks – the festival's guest of honour, head juror and the focus of the festival's retrospective – holding court. This was of course during the Franco period – I can recall buying the *International Herald Tribune* there daily, and discovering on occasion that articles had been scissored out of every copy. And the degree to which the festival hospitality served as propaganda for a repressive regime – which was already evident when I had to pass through a ridiculously lavish spectacle on the grand stairway of an old opera house on my way out of the gala screenings, all the other exit doors being locked – became most apparent to me on the last day of the festival, when my passport was stolen (a frequent occurrence, I heard, due to San Sébastian's relative proximity to the French border). This actually proved to be a stroke of good fortune for me, because during the day it took me to acquire a replacement passport at the US embassy in Bilbao, the sweetness of the festival staff in helping me out included at least two or three trips to the local police station, where I wound up getting to witness a lot of what the festival for the previous ten days had successfully strived to keep invisible. (In all fairness, though, I should note that the festival's hospitality was no less lavish when I returned there in 1987, a dozen years after Franco's death.)

★ ★ ★

I estimate that up through the fall of 2007, I've attended roughly 165 film festivals in 41 separate venues. But during the 1980s, I was still mainly getting my feet wet. Apart from my second visit to San Sébastian, this mainly included starting to attend the Toronto festival on an annual basis in 1981 (when I was invited to programme a then-regular sidebar called 'Buried Treasures', which included that year the North American premieres of the director's cuts of Fritz Lang's Indian films and Elaine May's *Mikey and Nicky*); visits to the Denver Film Festival in 1983 and 1989 (initially to promote my book *Film: The Front Line*, published by the Denver-based Arden Press); starting to attend the Rotterdam Film Festival on an almost-annual basis in 1984; starting to attend the Chicago International Film Festival regularly in 1987 (shortly after I moved to Chicago from Santa Barbara to start reviewing films for the *Chicago Reader*, where Chicago film festival coverage was a major part of my job); the San Francisco Film Festival for the first time in 1988; and both the US Film Festival (as a juror) in Dallas and Berlin (for the first of three times) in 1989.

★ ★ ★

I'm proud to say that I was the first member of the American press ever invited to the Rotterdam festival, and I owe this privilege to the friendly intervention of Sara Driver and Jim Jarmusch, whom I'd known ever since I devoted a chapter of my *Film: The Front Line* to Sara. At that time, practically the entire event was held in a building called the Lantaren (which still functions today as one of the festival venues), where I recall attending press conferences with Joseph L. Mankiewicz (who was receiving the Erasmus Award that year), Raúl Ruiz (whose films I was seeing for the first time) and Philippe Garrel (who was showing *Liberté, la nuit*). This was a festival that soon became my overall favourite – at least until it was briefly supplanted by the Buenos Aires Festival of Independent Film during the four years (2001–04) it was directed by the film critic Eduardo Antin (better known as Quintín), about which I'll have more to say a bit later.

Part of what was special about Rotterdam was its semi-clandestine atmosphere – undoubtedly linked in part to the awful winter climate in late January and early February (the damp chill, often accompanied by rain and/or fog) as well as to the off-the-beaten-track nature of many of its films, not to mention other factors, such as the fact that one of the main festival hotels, the Centraal, had served as Gestapo headquarters during the Nazi occupation, or the fact that it was relatively easy to get stoned on grass before some screenings (a practice I'd already cultivated as a cinephile in New York during the 1960s and Cannes during the 1970s).

★ ★ ★

My first encounters with many countries have come about through accepting invitations to film festivals, and this has many clear advantages as well as certain drawbacks in getting acquainted with foreign cultures. My first visit to Asia, for instance, was as a juror at the Asian Pacific Film Festival, held each year in a separate country. The year I went, 1991, it was in Taipei, and I wound up as the only non-Asian member of a jury that included, if memory serves, three Taiwanese members (including critic Peggy Chiao, the head of the jury) as well as Stephen Teo (a specialist in Hong Kong cinema) and Aruna Vasudev (the India-based editor of *Cinemaya*). This alone provided a kind of crash course in Taiwanese culture that I very much appreciated; it often meant often going out to dinners where Mandarin was the only language spoken apart from a few occasional English remarks addressed to me and/or Aruna, which had the advantage of making me feel like I wasn't a tourist.

Most of our work was carried out over eleven days in a private screening room – the public screenings only started after we made our selections, coinciding more or less with the Golden Horse Awards – and to save time we were often presented with Taiwanese takeout lunches to eat in the dark, during which I could neither see nor identify most of what I was eating. There were also some wonderful touristic outings to Buddhist temples and the Royal Palace Museum as well as other memorable experiences – including a special screening of *Banana Republic* arranged for me by Peggy (specifically for its insights into the existential dilemmas of being exiled from mainland China), as well as a proper Chinese banquet attended by everyone from Chen Kaige to Wong Kar-wai, a late-night meeting with John Berry and Pierre Rissient at a jazz disco called the Blue Note, and an all-night party with cognac and karaoke thrown by Hou Hsiao-hsien at another club. My point, really, is that all these experiences made me feel I was learning something about the culture of the country I was visiting – unlike the usual circumstances attending most film festivals, which virtually guarantee being shut out of most aspects of everyday life and remaining inside a relatively autonomous dream bubble. But perhaps the biggest lesson of all, involving the highly interactive nature of the global Chinese diaspora and how quickly information could be exchanged within this network – something that became no less evident via fax machines during the Tiananmen Square demonstrations a few years later – came about a week after I returned to

Chicago from Taipei. A waiter at a Chinese restaurant asked me if I'd attended the Golden Horse Awards; when I asked him in stupefied response how he could have possibly known that, he explained that he'd just seen me appear briefly in a video distributed in Chicago's Chinatown.

I luckily visited Taipei at a peak time for Chinese and Taiwanese art cinema; among the films I saw there for the first time were the long versions of *A Brighter Summer Day* and *Actress* (both of which were, I believe, receiving their world premieres at the Golden Horse) as well as *Days of Being Wild*. But I could cite a few other festivals that I was often happier to attend for where they were located than for what they were showing: those held in Austin (South by Southwest, 2001–02 and 2005; Cinematexas, 2001), Dallas (the USA Film Festival, 1989), Hong Kong (2000), Honolulu (1990), Savannah (2001–03), Tehran (the Fajr Film Festival, 2001) and Valdivia, Chile (2007). If memory serves, during the four or so pleasant and friendly days I spent at the Thessaloniki International Film Festival in 1993, I found I had to devote more of my time to tracing the bureaucratic steps needed to acquire my return ticket to Chicago than I was able to spend seeing any films, including those at the Jules Dassin retrospective being held there that year.

Serving as a jury member in Tehran and Valdivia, I didn't get to sightsee quite as much as I would have liked, but I still found certain ways to get tastes of Iranian and Chilean culture. Curiously, I found that I was repeatedly asked the same question by locals at each festival. In Tehran, the question was, more or less, with a few variations, 'Is the reason why Americans like Iranian films so much because they show so many poor people, which is the way they like to view Iranians?' After awhile, I developed a boiler-plate response: 'Maybe it's true that Iranian films show too many poor people. But American films show too many rich people, so you're getting just as distorted a picture of my country as I'm getting of yours.'

In Valdivia, the question was much simpler and asked without much variation, and this one I found virtually impossible to answer: 'What do you think of the Chilean film industry?' (For me, this was tantamount to asking a Chilean who was visiting Chicago, 'What do you think of the American postal system?')

When I visited Tehran, Mehrnaz Saeed-Vafa, with whom I was co-authoring a book on Abbas Kiarostami at the time, was also visiting from

Chicago. It turned out that we both had only one opportunity to see a work print of Kiarostami's latest film, *ABC Africa*, at his own home, along with a few others, around 6 pm, near the end of the festival, almost immediately after my jury was supposed to complete its deliberations (i.e., by around 5 pm – it often takes about an hour to drive anywhere in Tehran). The potential problem with this plan, however, was that one of my fellow jurors, the Hungarian filmmaker Béla Tarr – an anti-cinephile with a vengeance, and also a friend – didn't like any of the films we saw, and found reasons to object to every film proposed for a prize. And even though our meeting started around ten in the morning, by around 4 pm it was beginning to look like I wouldn't make the screening of *ABC Africa* unless I could think up some radical ruse for preventing Béla from continuing his filibuster. So, when Béla left the room briefly for the toilet, I seized the opportunity by proposing that we vote right away on a slate of prizes – basically a list that granted some recognition of the favourite film of each juror (apart from Béla) – and my motion passed before he returned. The most interesting consequence of this was that, if memory serves, Béla wasn't even irritated by my ruse, which suggested that he may have been as trapped by his intransigence as the rest of us were.

One final anecdote, about the festival's closing-night ceremony. As someone who tends to dress up as infrequently as I can manage to (I had a black suit made while I was in Taipei that I've tended to use ever since), I hastily packed black dress shoes for this occasion, only to discover a couple of hours before it was time to put them on that I had somehow managed to pack two right shoes and no left one. So I was faced with a difficult choice: either wear the yellow Nikes I'd also brought along to Tehran or limp through the evening on two right shoes. I opted for the former, and later was told that no one objected; it was assumed that wearing tennis shoes to a formal event was a quaint American custom, regarded as chic in the US.

★ ★ ★

What was special about Quintín's four years of running BAFICI, which started a decade later, was the front-and-centre importance film criticism was made to have in almost every aspect of the planning, including the programming. I had already become friends with Quintín and his partner Flavia de la Fuente during my first visit to Buenos Aires the previous September, when the local chapter of FIPRESCI (the international film critics organisation) had invited me to give a series of lectures and Quintín and Flavia had hosted much of my stay, and helped arrange a lengthy interview for the local film magazine *El amante cine*. Then, after Quintín had been appointed director of this relatively new (and city-run) festival in December, he decided to commission and publish a Spanish translation of my latest book, *Movie Wars*, which had only just appeared in English – a somewhat radical decision insofar as I found a copy of *Les Guerras del Cine* in my hands when I arrived at the festival, where I was also serving on the competition jury, only four months later. (When a subsequent Chilean edition was brought out in Valdivia in 2007 – again with an index, and with a substitution of certain Chilean idioms and film titles for the Argentinian equivalents – this took little more than a month from initial proposal to a copy of the book in my hands, thereby giving the lie to all those bureaucratic American university presses that insist they need a year to carry our comparable projects.)

There were lots of experimental notions about festival programming being floated by Quintín during his four-year reign – not only lectures of various kinds (including ones where I presented, at various times, Forough Farrokhzad's *The House is Black* and Lewis Milestone's eccentric Depression musical *Hallelujah, I'm a Bum!* – the latter in an effort to engage with Argentina's then-ongoing Depression), clusters of films in various thematic categories, and an unusually large number of revivals of rare classics (most of them coming directly from the Paris Cinémathèque), but also a few notions that he never got around to trying out. (Perhaps the wildest of these was to hold all the jury's discussions and deliberations about the competition films in public, on a stage.) No less striking was his recognition of how crucial the social aspects of a film festival were by arranging to have a central 'meeting point', a café, at the location where most of the screenings were – a huge shopping mall named Abasto (the former site of the city's outdoor market), where one could often expect to find friends between films, and where various panels were also frequently held.

It was in the spirit of such principles that I proposed during my second year at the festival (when they published a Spanish edition of another book I was associated with – in this case a preliminary edition of an international collection I was co-editing called *Movie Mutations*) an annual programme, which I wound up presenting over the next couple of years, called 'Lost Cinema' (or, in Spanish, 'El club de las películas perdidas'). This consisted of inviting various filmmakers, critics and programmers to select a film that was virtually impossible to see, and sometimes even illegal to show, screening it in a video format and then discussing it with the audience. The screenings were free and the selections weren't mentioned by title in the festival catalogue (I encouraged the programmers to write descriptive hints about the films instead – and, in some cases, to convey the film's title to interested parties strictly by word of mouth). The basic idea was to try to approximate the conditions of showing rare works to your friends in your living room. And even though Quintín was initially somewhat skeptical of the whole idea, he let me try it out, and the results were pretty successful (even if the settings used each year – a screening room at Abasto and an auditorium at a nearby arts centre – were, by necessity, more institutional than I would have liked). The participants, apart from myself both years, were Michael Almereyda, Thom Andersen, Frédéric Bonnaud, Eduardo de Gregorio, Sara Driver, John Gianvito (whose first feature, *The Mad Songs of Fernanda Hussein* – which I'd initially seen at South by Southwest – won the first prize the year I was on the jury), Hans Hurch (director of the Viennale), Kent Jones, Ron Mann, Adrian Martin, David Oubiña and Mark Peranson.

If the series had continued for a third year, two filmmakers who had already agreed to participate were Claire Denis and Harun Farocki. But I'm happy to report it was later revived, at least in spirit, in Valdivia, when critic Gonzalo Maza proposed that I put on a similar one-shot programme of my own. I wound up showing two scarce Orson Welles items on video, both made around the same time as *Touch of Evil* – his unsold, half-hour TV pilot *The Fountain of Youth* and a fully edited but silent sequence from his *Don Quixote* featuring Patty McCormack, Francisco Reiguera and Akim Tamiroff, set inside a movie theatre.

★ ★ ★

Postscript:

The problem with any survey of memories of this kind is that it could be spun out indefinitely. But realising how much I've omitted, I'd like to conclude by listing, in chronological order, a dozen more especially vivid snapshot recollections. Over half of these involve meeting people, so I hope I can be forgiven for all the name-dropping.

- Meeting both Julia Solntseva (Alexander Dovzhenko's widow) and Marie Seton (Eisenstein's first English-language biographer) at the London Film Festival in 1975. (The latter's two favourites at the festival, she told me, were *Salo* and *In the Realm of the Senses*.)
- In 1989, getting to see the world premiere of the finished print of Jacques Rivette's 12-hour *Out 1* (1971) in Rotterdam with only four or five other people, over a series of days, as successive reels arrived from France.
- In 1990, getting to see Japanese films with Japanese audiences at the Honolulu film festival, where all the screenings were free to the public, and overhearing a couple of homeless street people give a rundown of their favourites at the previous year's festival.
- In 1996, my penultimate year on the selection committee of the New York Film Festival, I was invited by Godard to participate in a panel discussion about his *Histoire(s) du cinéma* in Locarno that would occur roughly halfway through our marathon viewing session in New York, in early August. In deference to Godard, I was kindly allowed to accept the invitation and fly to Locarno for just a weekend – during which time I was also able to see most of the early shorts of Abbas Kiarostami at a retrospective of his work and also see, for the first time, my favourite Iranian film, Farrokhzad's *The House is Black*. As it turned out, Godard didn't arrive until a day or so after I left, but the panel itself – which also included Florence Delay, Shigehiko Hasumi and André S. Labarthe – was memorable. (I hadn't been able to join the other three in Rolle, Switzerland a few days earlier to view an *avant-première* of chapters 3a and 3b, but this ultimately led to an even more exciting experience: a little over a year later, Godard brought both these chapters as well as 4a to the Toronto festival, where he showed all three to me in his hotel room.)

- In 1997, attending the Midnight Sun Film Festival in Sodankyla, Finland, far above the Arctic Circle, where I was present at the renaming of the town's main street as Samuel Fuller's Street (he had died the previous fall), and where I subsequently got to meet both Terry Gilliam and Chris Marker.
- A long dinner with Anna Karina and her father-in-law, John Berry, at the Viennale in 1998, with Ben Gazzara and Luc Moullet (among others) seated at the same table.
- A free outdoor concert by Emir Kusturica and the No Smoking Orchestra, Pesaro in 2000.
- In Weisbaden, 2002, a series of private screenings organised by a friend from Munich, Hans Schmid, to select a slate of festival winners, along with (among others) film distributor Margaret Deriaz and film director Mike Hodges.
- Later the same year, serving on the FIPRESCI jury at the Brisbane International Film Festival in Australia, and, immediately after awarding our prize to a particular favourite, Seijun Suzuki's *Pistol Opera*, going directly to a cybercafé, where I was able to order a DVD of the film from Japan.
- In 2005, meeting Betsy Blair at Il Cinema Ritrovato in Bologna.
- Locarno again, in 2005: after attending a Welles conference held in the middle of a massive Welles retrospective, one of the other participants, magician Abb Dickson, and I found ourselves stranded an extra day before we could fly back to the US, which enabled us to get better acquainted, and afforded me a chance to see several more of his tricks.
- In 2006, my second look at *Out 1*, this time with English subtitles, presented by Mark Peranson in Vancouver, who brought the just-arrived Pedro Costa to greet the two dozen or so survivors as soon as it was over.

IV.

THE FILMMAKER'S PERSPECTIVE

A Director on the Festival Circuit: An Interview with Atom Egoyan

RICHARD PORTON

Atom Egoyan is an archetypal case of a filmmaker whose career has been shaped by his intimate association with a host of film festivals. Several festival venues have been constants as Egoyan progressed from being a scrappy director of 'art films' to an international figure. The Toronto International Film Festival (located in the city where Egoyan has resided since his university days) screened his first feature, Next of Kin, *in 1984. TIFF has subsequently showcased virtually all of Egoyan's major projects;* Ararat *opened TIFF in 2002 and his latest feature,* Adoration, *was screened at the 2008 festival.*

Despite this home town recognition, however, Wim Wenders' decision to turn over his prize money for Wings of Desire *to Egoyan at the Festival du Nouveau Cinéma in Montreal in 1987 became a legendary film festival moment. In addition, after* Family Viewing, *the film that inspired Wenders' impromptu act of generosity, Egoyan became a fixture on the festival circuit. 1989's* Speaking Parts *marked Egoyan's first appearance at Cannes' Directors' Fortnight; he resurfaced at the same sidebar in 1991 with* The Adjuster. *From* Exotica *(1994) to the present, most of Egoyan's high-profile fiction films (as opposed to occasional smaller projects such as the too-little known documentary,* Citadel, *2006) have been showcased in competition at Cannes, although* Ararat *was shown out of competition, in the main selection, at the director's*

169

Next of Kin, Egoyan's first film, was screened at the Toronto International Film Festival.
(Photo: © Ego Film Arts)

request. The trajectory from a slightly outré marginal figure to a mainstream interna-
tional auteur perhaps culminated in the special Grand Jury Prize he received for The
Sweet Hereafter *in 1997. His one attempt to make an entirely mainstream film,*
Where the Truth Lies (*shown in competition in 2005*) *met with a scathing critical*
reception that may have made him reflective but has not left any visible psychic wounds.
In any case, Egoyan is no longer exclusively a filmmaker – and is as likely to surface as
a video artist engaged in gallery installations, or a director of opera (his production of
Richard Strauss's Salome *premiered in Toronto and went on to revivals in Vancouver*
and Houston) or theatre (his stage adaptation of Samuel Beckett's television play, Eh
Joe, *won acclaim in Dublin, London and New York.)*

In the following interview, Egoyan assesses his festival experiences – whether as
youthful spectator, aspiring filmmaker or, as his career reached maturity, jury member
– with an analytical, often humorous, eye.

Richard Porton: Although this volume is made up primarily of contributions by critics and filmmakers, I also think it's important to have a film-

maker's perspective. You seemed like the ideal person to interview since festivals – perhaps beginning with the screening of *Next of Kin* at the Toronto Film Festival – have provided you with many important career touchstones.

Atom Egoyan: Yes, I've been thinking about this lately. I was hugely invested in projecting the meaning of what these festivals meant – and that became a large part of how my journey through these events has marked me. The Toronto Film Festival was something I was keenly aware of as a student. I had seen filmmakers present their work there and I had covered the festival as a student journalist. I certainly fantasised about what it must have meant to be able to present a film at Toronto and have that kind of exposure. Likewise, many of the films I'd admired at that time were European movies that included the prizes they had garnered at various festivals in the presentation credits. You wouldn't only see Cannes and Berlin; you might also see Locarno and these other moments in a film's career that took on a special significance.

That was part of my make up at that time: to dream of what it would be like to be part of one of these hallowed events. It wasn't an immediate process for me, though. *Next of Kin* made it to some festivals – but nothing remarkable outside of Toronto and Mannheim. *Family Viewing* was submitted to Cannes and wasn't invited; it was also submitted to Locarno during the summer of '87 and wasn't invited. It then premiered in Toronto and was invited, with some hesitation, to the Forum in Berlin. And then it was invited to Locarno the following summer – at which point I discovered that it hadn't even been properly submitted to Locarno the first time. The then-director of the festival hadn't even seen it. So there's a whole level of machination that goes on in terms of selection and one's entry into the selection process that is very daunting and mysterious to a filmmaker at the beginning of his career. You're at the mercy of people who can champion your work and put it through.

RP: The festival circuit is usually posited as the antidote to the mainstream. And Wim Wenders's decision to honour *Family Viewing* by handing over his prize money to you during the Festival du Nouveau Cinéma in Montreal is often cited as a key turning point in your career.

AE: For me – at that point – the festival was the mainstream. I really didn't have a sense of what the mainstream meant outside of the festival circuit. It was a different moment, perhaps. But it was long before *sex, lies, and videotape* and long before making an indie film became a ticket to success.

The experience at the Festival du Nouveau Cinéma was every young filmmaker's fantasy, a remarkable moment where I was able to achieve a degree of visibility because of Wim's generosity. In retrospect it seems almost choreographed. But it was in fact a great surprise, which focused attention on a film that might not otherwise have had any.

RP: And it's become a seminal event in almost every biographical sketch or piece of journalism devoted to your career.

AE: For a while, the weight of it was almost oppressive. I actually did an open forum on that event and dissected it, eventually coming up with the conclusion that Wim hadn't even seen the film at that point. The film had received an honourable mention and he made a gesture by giving me the cash prize. Then a screening was convened and he supported it although I always wonder what might have happened he had first seen the film and hated it. Nevertheless, it's remarkable that festivals can create those moments and the public can share in the fantasy. This kind of passing on of the baton can only really resonate if the public is attuned to the experiences of these filmmakers – and what these films mean. There was a tone and a space at the festival which allowed this to happen and I'm not sure it could happen again. Wim was also the head of the jury at Cannes when Soderbergh won the Palme d'Or for *sex, lies, and videotape*. There was also a feeling that this was a special moment. But it's not a given.

RP: So you thought of yourself as more of an experimental filmmaker at that time?

AE: Those films were made with arts council grants and there were no expectations that they would perform commercially.

RP: There was no funding through Telefilm?

AE: *Next of Kin* and *Family Viewing* were arts council projects. I had rejected Telefilm. They had approached me, but the use of video – shooting it as a live TV show and then transferring it – was something that fell outside of their realm of understanding. It was an experimental work – using narrative devices of course – and was not a Telefilm project.

RP: And, to a certain extent, you've continued to alternate between relatively mainstream projects and more experimental work.

AE: Now I find myself in a strange place where I can make a small film, like the project *Citadel*, which I made a few years ago. I can be incredibly selective. I really haven't shown it at any festivals at all because it wasn't meant to be a commercial project and was made with no budget whatsoever. There's no expectation, or pressure, for it to perform commercially. So I prefer to see it as a purely artisanal project. I don't necessarily view festivals in the same way as I once did. It may be the product of my age or the point I've reached in my career. But I tend to see them now more as marketplaces than forums.

RP: Since I saw you present *Citadel* at the Barbican in London, I know that you wanted to appear with the film to answer questions at selected screenings. I suppose it would be too arduous to do this at numerous festivals.

AE: Maybe if it was something I had made twenty years ago, I would have devoted time to traveling with the film. It's funny – there was a retrospective of my work at the Pompidou last year – and it seemed to make sense in that context. If one wants to look at the film festival as a forum for discussion, it almost assumes that the filmmaker will be present. *Citadel* in particular is a work that can't be shown without some kind of discussion.

RP: So, although *Citadel* is a film that you couldn't imagine within the commercial realm, it hasn't (with the exception of Hot Docs in Toronto) screened on the festival circuit.

AE: Yes, although we did screen it several years ago at this small digital venue that I set up in Toronto and it proved ideal for this project. In terms of having a discussion, I think the most successful festival experiences I've had have been at the Forum in Berlin and certainly at the Festival du Nouveau Cinéma in Montreal.

RP: Didn't the Rotterdam Film Festival help to launch *Calendar*, a similarly 'small film'?

AE: That's a very interesting festival story. *The Adjuster* won the grand prize at the Moscow Film Festival in 1991. Part of that prize was a million rubles to make a film in the Soviet Union. The result of this was that I went right from Moscow to Armenia with the idea of organising a plan

In 1991, *The Adjuster* screened at the Directors' Fortnight in Cannes and won the grand prize at the Moscow Film Festival. (Photo: Courtesy of Johnnie Eisen/© Ego Film Arts)

to make a film. Within the next year, with the fall of the Soviet Union, the ruble was devalued to the point where it was practically worthless. It was quite shocking; on the strength of this prize I went to what was then still a Soviet republic only to find that all the funding had evaporated. I went to the CineMart in Rotterdam, where we were required to tell a story about our projects. Fortunately, almost miraculously, a producer, Doris Hepp at ZDF, offered $100,000 to resurrect this project. Since this film was born out of a festival prize that then eluded me and was then resurrected at another festival, I suppose it could be termed the quintessential festival film – born in one, revived in another, and then premiered at yet another festival the following year – the Forum in Berlin.

RP: Of course, by now you've also had a great deal of exposure at Cannes, a dizzying marketplace and thereby radically different from festivals such as Rotterdam and Locarno.

AE: There was a point in my career, after *Speaking Parts* got into the Directors' Fortnight, when I began to feel that I was on a completely different track. My alignment with Alliance eventually became married to the idea of presenting my films at Cannes as a springboard for sales. That became true with *The Adjuster*, which was also included in the Fortnight the following year. *Calendar* was a very interesting film from this perspective. That film was seen as a bit of a deviation since Alliance was not excited about the film's prospects as a commercial property. And, although they ended up representing it, their concentration at that time was on *Exotica* – a film that was already in the works – which they thought could be a breakthrough.

RP: And *Exotica* was a competition film, wasn't it?

AE: It was invited into the competition at the last minute. It was originally included in Un Certain Regard. We held back since it was previously invited for the Fortnight. It was then of course bumped up to the competition.

RP: I've attended Cannes since 2001 and, although most of the mainstream critics flock to the competition films, I find that much of the truly interesting work is included in Directors' Fortnight.

AE: Well, after a while it's a purely commercial decision. Here's another interesting festival story. The last film, *Where the Truth Lies*, was not intended for Cannes at all. But the selection committee insisted on seeing it although we were very hesitant. Although I usually like to send a print, we sent a tape. They were very adamant about showing the film. It's very difficult to decline an offer after you go through that system and I think we were also suddenly intrigued by what this might mean. And I think you might also lose your sense of how a film should be positioned. It's exciting; there's a momentum that happens with that particular festival. But it's still an open question as to whether it was a smart idea to screen that film at Cannes. From a commercial point of view, and that of international sales, it was spectacularly successful. And the reviews that came out the first day, particularly the one in *The Hollywood Reporter*, were over the moon. So we thought we had certainly made the right choice. But then there was the flip side and we were sort of pummeled by other critics. But, by that point, the sales had already been made. That's how quickly things move. It's very strategic and has to be done carefully. And, of all the markets where the film screened, France was the only country where it performed well. So perhaps the point is that, although we think of these festivals as international events, they're also *national* events (and this is true of Cannes as well). Cannes serves as a national platform and that's true of many other festivals; one thinks of Berlin and Venice, for example. A premiere at either of those festivals is purely of importance for European distribution; for a premiere of a North American film to matter over here it has to be aligned with a screening at the Toronto festival. At least at Cannes you do get international exposure.

RP: Moving on to another topic, did it bother you that the press made much of the fact that David Cronenberg was head of the jury when *Felicia's Journey* was screened at Cannes? Do you think they were trying to whip up a rivalry between two Canadian directors?

AE: David is my mentor and I have tremendous respect for him. Having headed a jury myself at Berlin, I know there are certain decisions that no one will understand outside the confines of a room. David and I happen to be two prominent directors from Canada. There was really quite unrealistic speculation, which probably wouldn't have occurred if we were from any other countries. This certainly wouldn't have happened if we were from the United States.

I was on the jury at Cannes the year Cronenberg's *Crash* was shown and was a very vocal supporter of the film. It was a fractious – in fact publicly fractious – jury. I made a very public bid for that film – not to support David per se but to support what I thought was a very extraordinary piece of work, an exceptional film. You hope to put your personal allegiances aside and focus on the work. I can't presume to know what anyone on that jury thought of *Felicia's Journey*. I never really talked about it with David.

I say this with some perspective. I think it's important to talk about the fact that, from a filmmaker's point of view, it's very deforming when you're going through an event like Cannes. You're in a very strange bubble for those ten days. You don't see the other films and you're talking endlessly about your own work. So you're divorced from any reality of what the other competition films are like. Everyone is telling you that your film is the best they've seen – and they might be doing that either sincerely or maliciously. But, for whatever reason, because of your state

The Sweet Hereafter **won the Grand Jury Prize at the 1997 Cannes Film Festival. (Photo: Courtesy of Johnnie Elsen/© Ego Film Arts)**

of mind, you might be prone to believe that. It becomes very exaggerated. So, when you reach the evening when the prizes are announced, it can be quite devastating.

RP: Well, Angelopoulos was quite visibly upset one year at Cannes when he didn't win the Palme d'Or he thought he deserved.

AE: It gets a little ugly because people are in a very peculiar zone. For those ten days, that is the world. It takes some time away from it for the dust to settle and learn to look at the experience objectively. It's a very particular community that congregates at a very strange town in the south of France to see some exceptional films as well as some films that probably don't have a right to be there at all.

RP: That would coincide with my perception of Cannes – although I assume screening *The Sweet Hereafter* there was one of your happiest festival experiences.

AE: It was an exceptional experience because it felt, in some ways, to be the culmination of so many things. It was the last film – before *Adoration* – I had produced myself. And I was working with a group of people, who had all quite beautifully made their way to Cannes to see various films, either in the Directors' Fortnight or in competition. So it was a very sweet evening. It felt like the right moment. I'll never forget when *Exotica* won the International Critics Award. I've always felt strange about it because that was the year that Kieslowski was there with *Three Colours: Red*, which walked away empty-handed.

RP: I suppose that example demonstrates the arbitrariness of many coveted prizes. What was your experience like as a member of the Cannes jury in 1996, the year *Secrets & Lies* won the Palme d'Or?

AE: And *Breaking the Waves* won the Jury Prize. It was an exceptional year. Of course, while there were exceptional films we acknowledged, there were also exceptional films that we weren't able to acknowledge. For example, we weren't able to acknowledge Aki Kaurismaki's *Drifting Clouds*. *Fargo* was also screened. It just wasn't possible to give awards to everyone.

I had an interesting experience because Coppola was head of the jury and he was certainly someone who I had mythologised. It was fascinating to see that cult of personality emerge and witness someone who had the most remarkable double hit at Cannes between *Apocalypse Now* and *The Conversation*, which both won the Palme d'Or. I think what was remarkable about his process was that he didn't think we should discuss the films at first but should instead get to know each other. The idea was that we would all know where we were coming from when we finally came to discuss the films. The idea was good in theory. But what happened was that we spent ten days socialising and being congenial while eventually discovering on the last day that we all had wildly different tastes. In fact, we should have started that work long before.

RP: Since the process seems so opaque to the clueless observer, it's interesting to hear these inside tidbits.

AE: Yes, every head of the jury has his own technique. Some presidents might want every film to be discussed while some might want to eliminate certain projects from discussion – if a film doesn't have any support on the jury, the argument goes, why discuss it? I think that's a dangerous approach because the discussions are what form the consensus.

RP: These decisions often seem based on personal whims or the ability of certain jury members to dominate the group. It's all quite unpredictable.

AE: For me, the most troubling aspect of a festival is that your experience of a film is set against what you've seen before and certainly what you're going to see next, not an isolated experience. One could argue that the ideal jury would be the one that had exactly the same experience of when those films are viewed: they should be watching them together at all times. And, since there might be the possibility of other projections that would alter that experience, they should watch *only* those films. The cumulative experience of a festival is alchemical. I've had incredible emotional responses to work that left me cold seeing them months later outside of that event. It's a peculiar aberration of how we normally view films.

RP: And perhaps the reverse is also true – films that seemed undistinguished during a festival can take on new resonances subsequently. Seeing five or six films a day and having very little to eat can obviously have an impact on your responses.

AE: And there are also personalities. You might have a very strange run in with someone that leaves you in a very bad way. Or you might be pushed around trying to get into a certain screening and that might leave a bad taste. So all of these things are unpredictable and can alter your perception of a film.

RP: Festivals such as Cannes and Toronto have now become so media driven and besotted with celebrities that the glitz often threatens to interfere with the experience of the films themselves.

AE: They become victims of their own success and I'm not sure there's any way to prevent that. One of the joys of the Toronto International Film Festival is that you can actually chart your way through the event and perhaps focus on some of the less-hyped films.

RP: Some people feel that Toronto has become too preoccupied with junkets and Hollywood premieres.

AE: But the wonderful thing about Toronto is that it presents so many varied festival events. You can make it a festival of Eastern European films or African cinema or experimental work. You can create your own festival. If you only focus on the studio releases, it could become unbearable. But I don't know why anyone would do that.

RP: When I was in Istanbul for the festival several years ago, I met several

Screened at Cannes and
Toronto in 2002, *Ararat*
remains Egoyan's most
controversial film.
(Photo: Johnnie Eisen/
courtesy of Serendipity
Point Films)

Turkish critics and academics who were very fond of *Ararat* and went against the grain of what one would have thought would be stereotypical Turkish responses to the film. Do you think screening the film in Turkey was a worthwhile idea?

AE: I've had as much negative reaction to *Ararat* from the Armenian community as I've had from the Turkish community. There are ambiguities in the work and it's designed to provoke a response. There was a very alarmist reaction to *Ararat*, mainly from people who hadn't seen the work. It was attacked as propaganda, which by its very nature has to be simple-minded and ham-fisted, and the film is anything but that. *Ararat* allows for a conversation to begin, and certainly the scene between the Turkish actor and the young boy observing the film production represents where I'm positioned. I was heartened by the Turkish intellectual response to the film. I've also had a similar response to a joint project I did with the Turkish video artist Kutlug Ataman that premiered in Toronto at the Luminato Festival and then was invited to the Istanbul Biennale. The problem is that there are nationalists who just have a knee-jerk reaction without giving much time to the work. That's just a result of our unfortunate history.

My work was represented at the Istanbul Film Festival quite early on with *The Adjuster* and *Exotica*, both of which received commercial distribution in Turkey. I toyed with the idea of going, but I wanted some assurance from the festival committees that I could enter the country and speak with a certain degree of openness. I never received confirmation that I could, for example, use the word genocide (although I remember a very open discussion with a Turkish journalist in Locarno that I found quite liberating). Even recently, with this current installation, I was asked to refrain from using the word genocide. I'm torn. On the one hand, I applaud the programmers' decision to show the work. On the other, I find it difficult to censor myself and feel constrained under those circumstances.

RP: To move from political constraints at festivals to more absurd confrontations – I recall a New York Film Festival Q & A for your film of *Krapp's Last Tape* where the notoriously nasty John Simon asked a string of obnoxious questions. That must be disconcerting for a filmmaker.

AE: I was there one year with my composer, Mychael Danna and he made the most wilting comments. I think it was the year that Mychael had composed the music for *The Ice Storm* and John Simon asked about how he felt about substituting 'exotic bells and whistles' for a soundtrack (laughs). He said it with the utmost casualness. With *Krapp's Last Tape*, as I recall, he asked why I made the most boring possible interpretation of that play. But it's all a bit of a performance for the benefit of a room full of other journalists. You become a bit hardened after a while.

RP: In the final analysis, how would you sum up the pluses and minuses of the festival experience?

AE: Given that I now have a body of work, I'd say that the festival circuit has been essential to introducing the public to that work. I'd say that, for certain types of films, festivals have become perhaps the only form of distribution. They were once seen as launching pads for films that might be picked up by a network of smaller distributors interested in experimental or offbeat work. But because of the financial precariousness of theatrical distribution for many films that should be seen on a large screen, the festival might be in fact the only form of distribution. For this reason, festivals have perhaps become even more valuable. For filmmakers who, for example, employ long takes and a certain leisurely rhythm, they deserve the best projection possible. And a good festival can at least offer optimal projection – if not the guarantee of commercial distribution.

The *Dekalog* Re-View

Each issue of *Dekalog* includes this 'Re-View' section where readers' feedback is edited by each edition's respective guest editors and published in subsequent editions.

All readers are therefore very much invited to participate in the discussions, or raise issues for debate as instigated by any of the contributions to the volumes in this series, by contacting any of the series' guest editors on the following email address: dekalog@wallflowerpress.co.uk

DEKALOG 1: ON THE FIVE OBSTRUCTIONS

A Response from Jørgen Leth

As an artist one sometimes experiences wise people's reading of one's work as a new kind of insight. New thoughts are traced out, thoughts that were certainly already in the work, but which one hadn't really fully developed oneself.

The Five Obstructions seems to require analysis, and as one of the film's makers I find it very fruitful that views have been sought from writers other than professional film scholars and critics. It is a film about making films, or about jump-starting a creative process, and as such it is the occasion for interesting thoughts about 'artistic nesting' (Paisley Livingston), that is, about works embedded within a larger work. Susan Dwyer (in 'Romancing the Dane: Ethics and Observation') goes in a quite different direction, in that she chooses to take Lars von Trier's idea about psychological therapy seriously.

She thinks that he gives me a way of understanding myself better. And perhaps even a way of taking my life in a more ethical direction as a result of this new self-understanding.

The film falls outside of conventional genres and it raises quite a number of tricky questions that are difficult to settle in any definitive way. I especially like theories that confirm or affirm something that does actually exist in the work, but is often overlooked. This is why I particularly value the line of thought, pursued by several of the contributors, which recognises the film as a creative game played by two grown men. Murray Smith takes up the film's playful dimension in 'Funny Games'. His matter-of-fact assertion that von Trier's references to therapy involve the assumption of a role, in much the same way that Dogme's evocation of monkish brethren did, is wonderfully liberating. In his essay 'Work and Play: The 5-0 Game', Trevor Ponech makes clear that while von Trier and I go into the sophisticated game with different starting assumptions, we share the expectation that the game – to be played according to strict rules – will be fruitful and will lead to new insights. If one has an experimental approach to filmmaking then one of course often finds oneself confronting a wall, something that has to be overcome; because the preference is to reinvent the grammar of film's language each time. Difficult circumstances are necessary if the creative process is to lead to something worthwhile. Exactly as in *The Five Obstructions*. Coming to understand that the creative process can be turned into a game is sometimes the solution. My film *Moments of Play* (*Det legende menneske*, 1986) begins with my poem entitled 'I'm Ready Now'. This poem articulates something like a credo on the topic and means a lot to me.

I really like Hector Rodriguez's essay 'Constraint, Cruelty and Conversation'. Rodriguez is right when he says that von Trier also has a ludic approach to filmmaking. This provides another interpretive filter for the work, and that's what's good about insightful film criticism. I find it particularly gratifying to see Rodriguez emphasise the film's set-up 'as a creative and open-ended adventure', and not least that he adds that this is the only model for filmmaking of any interest to him. He also provides a refreshing new angle on the concept of ambiguity. Based on the film, it is hard to see who dominates whom, and to distinguish the mask from the authentic self. In my view he really goes to the core of the matter when he says that 'the point of this indefiniteness is not ... to encourage viewers to "think for themselves". Rather the point is to express an image of thought, a paradigm of what it means to think.' And with reference to philosopher Gilles Deleuze he speaks about a 'radical openness without a predefined image' and concludes that 'the film tackles the possibility of thinking thoughts that defy clear-cut categorisation'.

Mette Hjort ('Style and Creativity in *The Five Obstructions*') and Peter Schepelern ('To Calculate the Moment: Leth's Life as Art') have an advantage in that they both know my work as a whole, and have written about aspects of it before. Hjort writes insightfully about the meaning of style (and stylisation), with references back to some of my other films. And Schepelern provides a context for understanding my debate-driven memoirs. Both identify some key threads that run through the films.

Hjort suggests a possible new study of my films, one that makes some sense now that the Danish Film Institute is putting out my entire work (45 films in all) in six DVD box sets. She suggests the value of a close reading of the countless art historical references, and of the constant return to elements of a minimalistic practice in my work. She points to the 'hidden' but often very direct inspiration that I've drawn from artists such as René Magritte, Edward Hopper, Bill Brandt and Andy Warhol, as well as from some of Jean-Luc Godard's scenes. In that sense the films have a tightly woven texture that calls for analysis, not least in relation to the artistic currents of the early 1960s, which went unnoticed by most film people in Europe.

I make films and I'm no philosopher. I even hold the view that it can be good, as an artist, to be a little stupid, a little naïve. I actually prefer it when the camera movements and the editing are slightly stupid. They certainly shouldn't be clever. I hate the image as illustrated thought. But this stance doesn't make me any less hungry for accounts of my work that help to shed light on my creative process. That's something I can use. I am fully aware of what the *Dekalog* publication does for the understanding of *The Five Obstructions*.

Jørgen Leth
15 September 2008

***

I came to Susan Dwyer's essay on *The Five Obstructions* whilst writing a long article on self-deception. In that article I distinguish between the ways first-, second- and third-person perspectives function with respect to self-deception. Though Dwyer doesn't actually use the term 'self-deception', her account of the second-person point of view, and of the modes of self-constitution it enables, sheds light on the self-deceiver's peculiar habits of evasive dependency. Dwyer is well aware of the first- person's inevitable vulnerability to the perspective of the Other, and of that perspective's possible epistemological consequences; but, like the film itself, she sees boundedness, limitation, as a gift that can potentially spare the Other some of the destructive effects of hubristic, monomaniacal self-assertion, whether in the arts or in 'life itself'. My article is a study of Lillian Hellman's memoirs, so I was particularly pleased to find a perceptive discussion of these matters which focused on another creative medium.

Richard Freadman, Lingnan University

***

I especially enjoyed the eye-opening article by Paisley Livingston showing how the aesthetic value of the five short films depends on the context in which they are represented, and the very informative and insightful article by Peter Schepelern analysing Jørgen Leth's complex and, for a period, much-discussed role as both an avant-garde artist and a public figure in Danish society. I also really appreciated the various 'bonus' features: a comprehensive list of festival appearances, thorough description of the origins of the project and the reception of the film, and finally the in-depth interview with Jørgen Leth containing all the relevant questions about the film's style, production and general philosophy. A splendid work that makes one look forward to the following volumes in the series.

Morten Egholm, University of Copenhagen

***

What I find especially useful in *Dekalog 1* is the analysis of Jørgen Leth's and Lars von Trier's collaboration in *The Five Obstructions*. This analysis allows for more general theorising about the interaction between constraints and creativity in the social field of filmmaking. The study of creativity within film and film production studies is crucial because it contributes to a shift from imaginaries centred on the autonomous auteur towards a more realistically based comprehension of the social, economic and technological conditions of creativity in film production.

In *Dekalog 1* the creative role of obstructions, rules and games is discussed in some depth, and some of the articles briefly touch upon their effect in terms of 'chance'. Chance and opportunity are essentially products of constraints, and von Trier and Leth consciously work with both as a means of fostering creativity. Thus, it could be fruitful I think, to further theorise the dynamics between types of constraints on the one hand and the construction of types of opportunity and chance, and the breaking of constraints on the other.

Cecilie Givskov, University of Copenhagen

DEKALOG 2: ON MANOEL DE OLIVEIRA

I was fascinated to read Fausto Cruchinho's article 'The Woman in the Shop Window and the Man Looking at Her: The Politics of the Look in Oliveira's Oeuvre'. It so happens that Manoel de Oliveira's latest film, *Eccentricities of a Blond Hair Girl*, premiered in Berlin in February this year, is precisely – and primarily – about a man looking at a woman framed in a window. This is a felicitous example of the way that artists can often belatedly provide literal confirmation of the metaphors that critics apply to their work.

Having recently written an overview of Manoel de Oliveira's work from a rather different, more journalistic perspective, I'm fascinated to read the more scholarly approaches to his films in *Dekalog 2*. The collection is extremely valuable for followers of the director's oeuvre, which – as several contributors point out – is elusive to the point of being virtually inaccessible, in terms of limited availability on DVD and rarity of screenings. The book's contributors impress in their attention to the complexities of an oeuvre which is too often dismissed as a glorious but eccentric and even inscrutable aberration in the field of European cinema. Relating Oliveira's work to the standard economics of film production, Randal Johnson notes the point that Oliveira's concept of film-making is idiosyncratic and at odds with the norms of filmmaking practice. But what is especially suggestive in several of these essays is that they emphasise Oliveira's literary and historical – rather than specifically filmic – interests, especially his working practices with the novelist Agustina Bessa-Luis. The inescapable conclusion: what makes Oliveira so distinctive as a filmmaker is that his works beg to be read not as an exotic or dissident form of cinema, but as a branch of literature pursued by other means.

Jonathan Romney, film critic, *Independent on Sunday*

***

Dekalog is shaping up to be a fascinating series. I like the sense of a focused conversation amongst the different contributors in each volume, and the opportunity to re-view the previous volume. The topics chosen so far all merit deeper exploration, particularly the 'cerebral cinema' of Manoel de Oliveira, whose neglect is symptomatic of a wider underappreciation, at least in the English-speaking world, of the incredible riches in Portugal's gorgeously anachronistic cinema. There are several fascinating and subtle close readings of de Oliveira's multifaceted films within these pages, but I was most grateful for Joao Benard da Costa's, himself one of the greatest living writers about film. His far-reaching study of the consistencies and ruptures within de Oliveira's oeuvre is a model of auteurist analysis, and ultimately points the reader where all good film criticism should, back to the films themselves.

Kieron Corless, Deputy Editor, *Sight and Sound*